NEW ZEALAND
ILLUSTRATED
atlas

Hodder Moa Beckett

AA GUIDE TO NEW ZEALAND ROAD RULES AND CONDITIONS

If you are from another country, it is very important that you take a little time to learn the local road rules and regulations — for your own and others' safety.

To help you do this, here is the most important information from the road code.

Driving Licences: *A current licence and/or international licence are acceptable.*

Minimum age for rental car hiring is 21 years.

Automobile Association: *The AA provides a road-map and breakdown service.*

Free reciprocal membership privileges are offered to members of equivalent overseas organisations.

Highways: *New Zealand highways are mainly of a high standard; most main highways are sealed and offer no difficulty for motorists from other countries. Those routes not sealed are generally well graded and maintained.*

Keep Left

In New Zealand, traffic travels on the left hand side of the road.

Speed Limits

Drive at a safe speed. Drive so you can stop short of the vehicle in front. On a country road with no centre line or lanes, drive so you can stop in half of the clear road you can see in front. On roads with centre line or lanes, drive so you can stop in the length of clear lane in front of you – be prepared to avoid obstructions in your lane.

New Zealand speed limits are in kilometres not miles.

You must not exceed **50 km/h** in all built up areas.

"OPEN ROAD" speed limits apply:
Cars, vans, motorcycles   100 km/h
Heavy motor vehicles   90 km/h
Vehicle towing trailer
or caravan   80 km/h

Do not exceed **50 km/h** where any of these makes a higher speed unsafe — bad weather, poor visibility, presence of children, pedestrians, cyclists, heavy traffic or slippery road surfaces. If none of these hazards are present the open road limit (100 km/h) applies.

Roundabouts

At a roundabout, signal if you wish to turn, give way to traffic on the right, and turn left into roundabout.

Overtaking

Overtake on the right except:
- when directed by a police officer
- when there are two or more lanes on your side and you can safely overtake on the left

Don't overtake near:
- a pedestrian crossing
- a railway crossing
- an intersection
- a blind bend, crest of a hill or anywhere else where you cannot see clearly at least 100 metres in front of you

Don't overtake in a no passing line area. This is shown by a solid yellow line on your side of the road. Advance warning of these is often given by a broken yellow line.

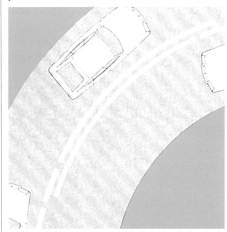

Where passing lanes are provided, move into the left lane unless overtaking.

Always turn on your indicator at least three seconds before you start to overtake.

Intersections

Slow down and look all ways, be ready to stop. If you are turning, give way to all traffic not turning and all right turning traffic coming from your right. Always obey both the traffic lights or signs, and the directions shown by words or arrows marked on the road.

If you need to change lanes, see that it is safe to move, signal for three seconds or more before you change lanes. Only change when you can do so safely.

When travelling straight through an intersection, give way to vehicles approaching on your right.

Always signal at least three seconds before you change lanes or direction and make sure it's safe to do so.

When turning right, give way to traffic travelling straight through in either direction. If two vehicles are both turning right, you must give way to the vehicle to your right.

When turning left, give way to traffic travelling straight through, and to traffic turning right into the road you wish to take.

Seat Belts

All modern vehicles are fitted with seat belts, front and back seats. In New Zealand it is compulsory to wear them. Failing to do this can incur a $75 fine.

Road Signs

You must stop completely, then give way to all traffic. There are two yellow lines on the road to help you stop in the right place.

Slow down, be ready to stop and give way to traffic not controlled by Stop or Give Way sign. There are white lines.

At traffic lights the following rules apply:

RED - means stop.
Note: North American, Canadian visitors
- you cannot turn left when stop light at an intersection is still red.

YELLOW - means stop.
If you are so close to the line that you cannot stop safely, keep going.

GREEN - means you can go if it is safe.

TOLL FREE EMERGENCY BREAKDOWN SERVICE

Don't Drink and Drive ...

Guidelines

Drink either

○ Female ● Male

¾ ❶	❺ 3½	2 ② 2¾	1¾ 2½
1 litre jug of beer	200ml glass of beer	330ml stubbie of beer	can of beer 4.5% alc/vol

④ 5½	3¾ 5½	1½ ②	1½ ②
low alcohol beer 2.0% alc/vol	single nip of spirits	335ml bottle of wine cooler	180 ml glass of wine

T̶LAND Transport
Waka Whenua

* These guidelines are for the first hour of drinking without food. If followed, they will keep a fully licensed driver under the legal limit. You should have no more than one standard drink per hour from then on. A standard drink is equivalent to 1 can of low alcohol beer, 1 nip of spirits, 1 glass of beer, 1/2 can or stubbie of beer, 1/2 bottle of winecooler or 1/3 of a glass (60 ml) of wine.

* Your limit may be less if you're smaller than average, unwell, taking medication or not used to alcohol. Drinking more than the amounts specified here will take you to a level considered dangerous and may take you over the legal limit.

* If you hold a learner or restricted licence your legal limit is much less. Therefore you shouldn't drink any alcohol before driving.

* Always eat when you drink to reduce the effects of the alcohol.

* Drink low alcohol beer (2.0 per cent or less) or non-alcoholic drinks to help keep you under the limit.

* Once you're over the limit, time is the only cure and this will only work if you don't drink more alcohol. Strong coffee, saunas, cold showers, walking or jogging won't get you back to the limit any faster.

* The legal limit for fully licensed drivers is 80 mg alcohol per 100 ml blood.

* Based on an average: male 67 kg, female 56 kg.

• From 1 April, 1993, stringent limits on drink driving with greatly increased penalties, were set for drivers under 20. Little more than one can of beer is now needed to put an averaged sized driver over the limit.

RED ARROW — stop and don't turn.

YELLOW ARROW — stop if you can safely.

GREEN ARROW — go and you have right of way.

Motorways

On a motorway you must not:
- walk or cycle
- stop your vehicle
- make a U turn

Keep to the left hand lane unless overtaking and always indicate at least three seconds before changing lanes.

Dangerous Roads

Confident drivers only.
* Beyond the Blue Lakes Car Park, Tasman Valley Road, Mt Cook.
* Skippers Canyon Road, Queenstown.
* 90 Mile Beach, Northland.
* Coast Road to Russell, Northland.
* Road to Milford Highway 94 Te Anau to Milford.

Slippery Road

Country Driving

New Zealand is a very beautiful country, and we are sure you'll love driving amongst our abundance of varied rural and alpine scenery. However, country driving needs special care, so be on the lookout for one-way bridges and unsealed roads which need to be approached with extra caution and care.

Narrow Bridge

One-Way Bridges

The circular "PLEASE GIVE WAY" sign with the large arrow for approaching traffic shows you must give way.

Please Give Way

The rectangular "RIGHT OF WAY" sign with the large arrow in your direction shows you have the right of way.

If you are travelling in the direction of the red arrow you must "GIVE WAY".

Right of Way

Parking Restrictions

When moving in or out of a parking space, always signal your intention before starting and watch out for passing traffic.

Do not park within 6 metres of an intersection, a pedestrian crossing or on a broken yellow line.

You may not park on this stretch of road between Monday to Friday at the times indicated.

Clearway 7am-9am Mon-Fri

The number under the "P" shows the maximum parking time allowed in minutes.

Failure to comply with these restrictions could result in your vehicle being towed away and impounded or in fines of up to $25 per hour.

P 30 Other Times

Pedestrian Crossings

When approaching a pedestrian crossing slow down and be prepared to stop.

Don't overtake anyone near a crossing and give way to any pedestrians on your half of the pedestrian crossing.

Crashes

If you are involved in a crash we advise you to do these things:-
1. Stop and help.
2. Do not admit to liability.
3. Obtain driver's name, address and insurance company of all other parties involved and the registration numbers of any other vehicles involved.
4. Report details to your Insurance Company within 24 hours and complete an accident report.
5. If someone is hurt report to the nearest police station within 24 hours.

0800 500 222

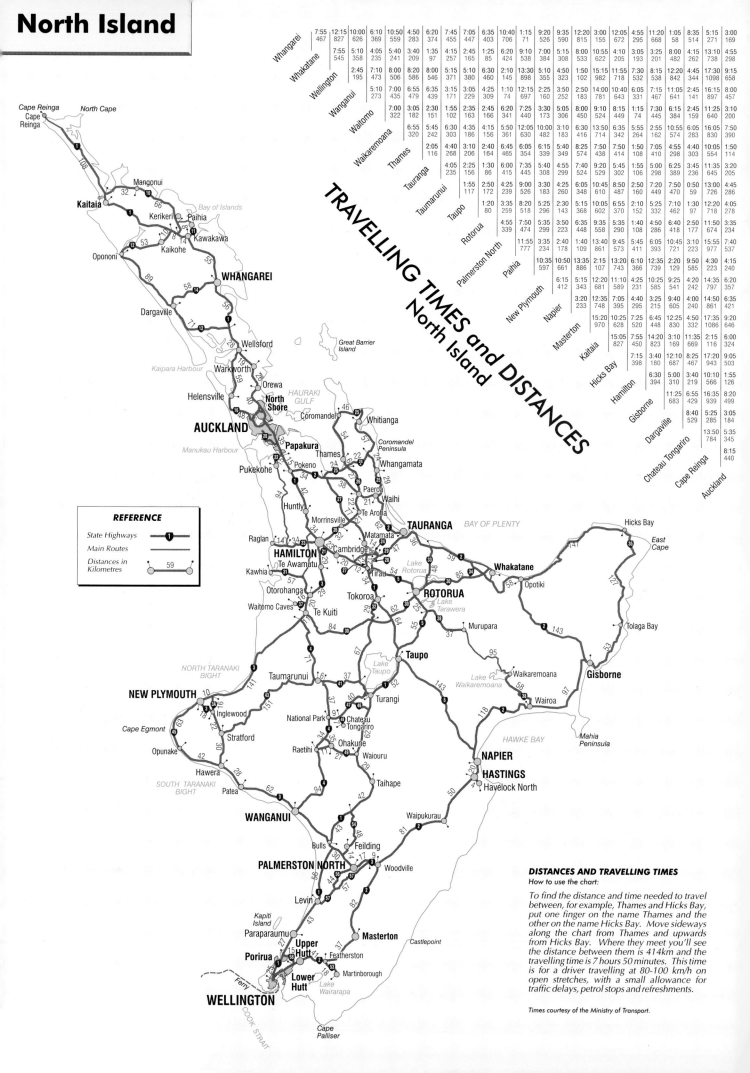

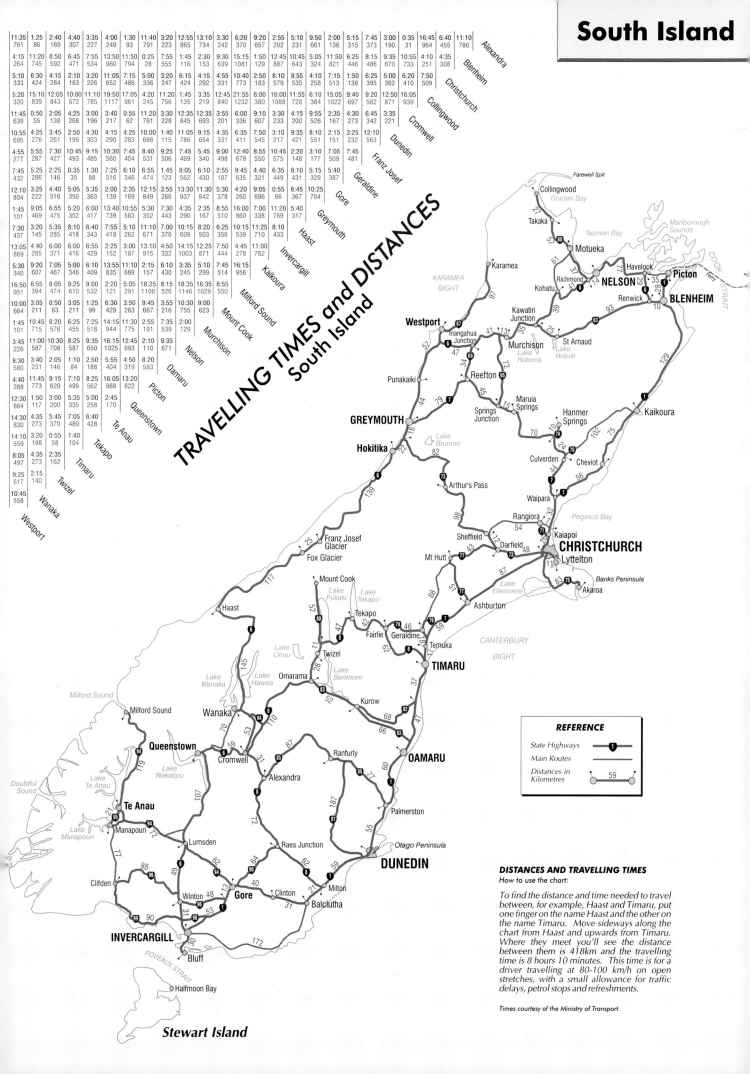

South Island

TRAVELLING TIMES and DISTANCES
South Island

REFERENCE

State Highways

Main Routes

Distances in Kilometres — 59

DISTANCES AND TRAVELLING TIMES

How to use the chart:

To find the distance and time needed to travel between, for example, Haast and Timaru, put one finger on the name Haast and the other on the name Timaru. Move sideways along the chart from Haast and upwards from Timaru. Where they meet you'll see the distance between them is 418km and the travelling time is 8 hours 10 minutes. This time is for a driver travelling at 80-100 km/h on open stretches, with a small allowance for traffic delays, petrol stops and refreshments.

Times courtesy of the Ministry of Transport.

Acknowledgments
The publishers wish to acknowledge the contribution
made by those who assisted with material for this atlas:
Department of Conservation
Statistics New Zealand
Local information centres thoughout the country.

Front cover photograph of Omarama courtesy of Deloitte Touche
Tohmatsu, from their specially commissioned Information Highway
Series, taken by John McDermott.

Back cover photograph of Sabine River, Nelson Lakes National Park
taken by Brian Enting, Key-Light Image Library Ltd.

ISBN 1-86958-641-7

© 1995 NZ Automobile Association, Inc.

DOSLI Map Licence PL097046/124

Cased edition first published in 1995
This limp edition published in 1997 by
Hodder Moa Beckett Publishers Limited
(a member of the Hodder Headline Group)
4 Whetu Place, Mairangi Bay, Auckland, New Zealand.

Reprinted 1998, 2000

Printed by Kyodo Printing Co. Pte Ltd, Singapore

Contents

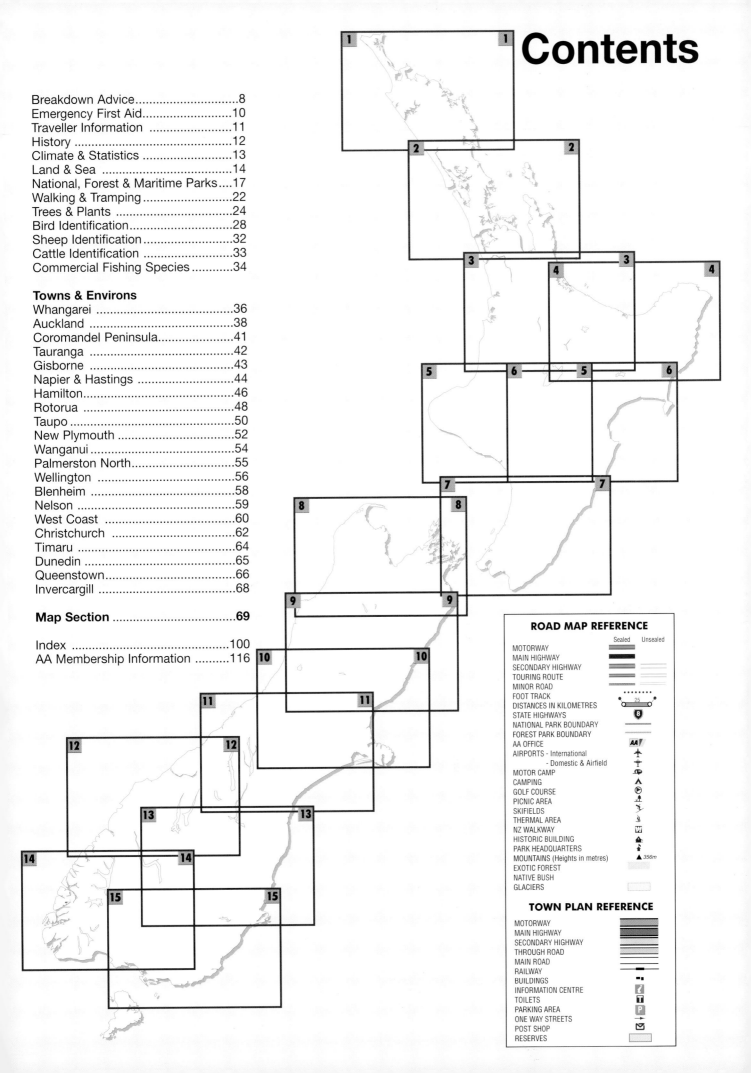

ROAD MAP REFERENCE

	Sealed	Unsealed
MOTORWAY		
MAIN HIGHWAY		
SECONDARY HIGHWAY		
TOURING ROUTE		
MINOR ROAD		
FOOT TRACK		
DISTANCES IN KILOMETRES		
STATE HIGHWAYS		
NATIONAL PARK BOUNDARY		
FOREST PARK BOUNDARY		
AA OFFICE		
AIRPORTS - International		
- Domestic & Airfield		
MOTOR CAMP		
CAMPING		
GOLF COURSE		
PICNIC AREA		
SKIFIELDS		
THERMAL AREA		
NZ WALKWAY		
HISTORIC BUILDING		
PARK HEADQUARTERS		
MOUNTAINS (Heights in metres)	356m	
EXOTIC FOREST		
NATIVE BUSH		
GLACIERS		

TOWN PLAN REFERENCE

MOTORWAY	
MAIN HIGHWAY	
SECONDARY HIGHWAY	
THROUGH ROAD	
MAIN ROAD	
RAILWAY	
BUILDINGS	
INFORMATION CENTRE	
TOILETS	
PARKING AREA	
ONE WAY STREETS	
POST SHOP	
RESERVES	

Breakdown Advice

The modern car engine is more reliable than its predecessors but it is also more complicated. A breakdown can occur with even the best-maintained cars – the way to minimise inconvenience is to be familiar with your car and be prepared.

Study the car handbook and the basic checklist on the right so that you are familiar with and can identify the most common causes of breakdown.

Breakdown tools and equipment

The toolkit supplied with your car is rarely adequate to cope with more than changing a tyre. When buying tools, buy no more than is necessary. First decide on the tools you intend buying. Make sure there is space in your car for a toolbox to be stored securely. If necessary drill and fit cleats so the toolbox can be held down firmly. A suggested list is as follows:

- tyre pump
- pliers
- adjustable wrench (large and small)
- open-ring spanners – 6 common sizes
- multigrips
- oil or dewatering lubricant
- clean rags
- tie-wire
- spark-plug spanner
- toolbox
- variety of screwdrivers
- plastic container for radiator water
- warning triangle
- jack and timber base
- wheelbrace
- insulating tape

What to do in case of a breakdown

Do not panic if your car breaks down. If the engine overheats, begins to 'miss' or even cuts out altogether, find somewhere that is safe to park clear of other traffic. Switch on the hazard warning lights and try to locate the problem.

If you must lift the bonnet, first place a warning triangle 50 large paces behind the car. If the car has overheated, wait until it cools before rectifying the fault. Do not attempt any work under the car when it is supported by a jack or parked on a slope.

A basic checklist

Petrol

If the car stops or will not start, you may have run out of petrol. In case the gauge is faulty, remove the filler cap and rock the car – there should be a sloshing sound if there is petrol in the tank. If the car has an electric fuel pump, switch on the ignition; if the tank is empty, you should hear a ticking sound.

A flooded engine

If you have flooded the engine trying to start it (there will be a strong smell of petrol), wait for 10-15 minutes. Some of the excess petrol will evaporate from the carburettor, especially if the engine is warm.

When you try again to start the engine, depress the accelerator slowly to the floor and keep it there; do not pump it. If you have a manual choke, do not use it until the engine fires, and not at all if the engine is still warm.

Rest the battery

Trying to start the engine is a big drain on the battery. If you have run the battery down switch everything off and let it rest for 15 minutes or so. The battery may recover enough power to get the car started again if there is nothing else wrong with the electrical system.

Overheating

If your engine has overheated, do nothing for at least 15 minutes while it cools; if you remove the radiator filler cap while the engine is very hot you could be scalded.

If there are no major leaks, you may get motoring again by topping the system up with warm water, and proceeding slowly while monitoring the temperature gauge. Never top up a hot motor with cold water.

Engine failure

Sudden and complete engine failure is often due to an electrical fault. A hesitant or stalling engine may be due to a fuel problem. A mechanical failure is generally accompanied by loud noises coming from the engine compartment. Declutch or select neutral and steer towards the edge of the road.

Tyre blowout

Slow down, braking very gently at first. Steer towards the left side of the road without making sudden movements of the steering wheel.

Brake failure

If the brakes fail without warning, do not apply the handbrake savagely. Decelerate and change back through the gears. Apply the handbrake with care, holding in the release button while doing so.

Jammed accelerator

Declutch or select neutral. Quickly depress the accelerator pedal several times. If this does not unstick the accelerator engage top gear or Drive and start braking against the power of the engine. Switch off the engine but do not turn the key to the steering lock position.

How to control an electrical fire

A fire under the bonnet may be caused by an electrical fault or leaking fuel. Your car's fire extinguisher should be within easy reach of the driver's seat. Slow down immediately and pull off the road. Apply the handbrake and select first gear or Park. Switch off the ignition and the electrical circuits, such as radio and headlights.

Pull the bonnet release. Stand at the front left side of the car and operate the

AA Toll Free Emergency Breakdown Service Phone 0800 500 222

Breakdown Advice

extinguisher through the gap under the bonnet rim. Do not open the bonnet as a sudden influx of oxygen may cause the fire to flare. If the fire cannot be put out, seek help. If there is a fire inside the car or under the dashboard, pull the bonnet release and get out of the car immediately. Disconnect the battery, then aim the extinguisher at the seat of the fire. Do not use liquid (BCF) extinguishers while there are people in the car.

What to do when the windscreen shatters

A laminated windscreen will not shatter. A stone thrown up will create a chip or large crack. The average older car has a toughened screen. If hit by a stone the screen crazes. Reduce speed and stop as soon as is practical and safe.

Place a blanket or jacket on top of the dash to prevent pieces of glass entering the heater demister. Place a blanket or piece of clothing over the ventilation ducts at the rear of the bonnet. Break the windscreen in the driver's view and remove any glass obscuring vision. Wind up all other windows.

Changing a wheel

Apply the handbrake and chock one of the wheels. Loosen the nuts by more than half a turn. Identify the correct jacking point. Place a plank under the jack if the car is on any surface other than tar or concrete. After changing the wheel, tighten the wheel nuts firmly, lower the car to the ground and further tighten the wheel nuts to their correct torque.

Clutch starting

In the event of starter or battery failure, a manual gear change car can be roll-started. With the ignition on, handbrake off, a gear such as second or third selected and clutch depressed, roll the car forward briskly. When the car is moving at about 15km/h – or as fast as the vehicle can be pushed – let the clutch out abruptly. When the engine starts, change into neutral and keep the engine running until it is warm.

Towing

Towing is not as easy as it looks and may even be illegal; for example on the Auckland Harbour Bridge, rigid or A-frame

towing is allowed but rope towing is not. Make sure there is a maximum of 4m between the two vehicles. Attach a towrope to a towbar, towing eye or part of either car's chassis.

Agree on a set of hand signals so that you understand what is going on. It is most important to keep the rope taut, so drive slowly until accustomed to this when changing gears. Watch the rope when turning corners and do not overrun it if it slackens. Position the towed vehicle slightly to the right of the towing vehicle so that the towed driver has a clear view ahead.

Warning

The trouble-shooting procedures described on these pages should be followed only if you are confident of carrying out a proper job on your car. If you have any doubts about your ability to find the fault and/or correct it, then do not go ahead but seek expert advice.

Jumper leads

If your battery is very low, a boost from another car battery may be all you need to get moving, and your own battery will be charged by your car's charging system.

Note that some cars with fully electronic ignition or fuel injection systems can be damaged by the sudden surge of current caused by connecting and disconnecting the jumper leads. Be guided by your handbook.

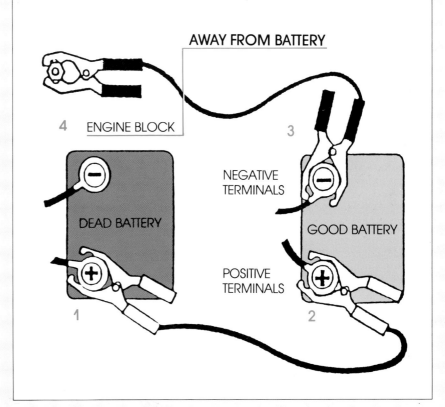

THE SAFE WAY to jump start a car.

Emergency First Aid

The AA recommends that all vehicles carry:

- A first aid kit
- A fire extinguisher
- Two safety triangles

1 Stop and look

- ❏ Slow down and pull over with caution.
- ❏ Park your car at a safe distance behind the accident.
- ❏ Turn on your hazard warning lights. At night light the scene with your headlights (if possible).
- ❏ If crashed vehicle is on fire, keep clear.

2 Warn other traffic

- ❏ Stop passing cars and send people up the road (with safety triangles, if available) in both directions. Get them to flag down oncoming traffic.

3 Immobilise crashed vehicle

- ❏ Ensure vehicle is safe, e.g. no downed power lines.
- ❏ Turn off ignition and remove keys.
- ❏ Check condition of casualties.
- ❏ Do not smoke – put out any cigarettes or pipes.

4 Call an ambulance

- ❏ Send someone off in each direction to phone (dial 111) for an ambulance and then tell them to come back to you. If no one is available, phone yourself, only if phone at hand.

Report
- Type of accident.
- Location.
- Number of injured.
- Unconscious or trapped victims – ambulance will inform police and fire service if needed.

5 Ensure casualties' safety

- ❏ Leave casualties in the position you find them in, unless they are in danger, e.g. busy roadway, fire.
- ❏ Get help to move victim.
- ❏ Lift by clothing – make sure one helper controls movement of head to make sure head position stays the same.
- ❏ If conscious casualty indicates loss of feeling in lower body or limbs, or has pain in neck or spine, DON'T move at all. Don't twist or turn victim.

6 Check casualties' breathing

- ❏ Loosen tight clothing at neck, waist and chest. Make sure the casualty can breathe freely.
- ❏ Check for regular breathing. If it stops, start mouth-to-mouth resuscitation.
  - Shake and shout.
  - Clear airway if necessary.
  - **Open the airway**
    Tilt head well back.
    Lift chin with fingers.
    Look, listen and feel for breathing.
- ❏ If breathing is absent begin rescue breathing:
  - Keep casualty's head tilted back.
  - Pinch nostrils.
  - Take deep breath, blow firmly with tight seal over victim's mouth.
  - Give two slow full breaths initially.
  - Chest must rise and fall.
  - If the chest does not rise, reposition the head tilt – chin lift.
  - Repeat resuscitation.

7 Treat casualties

Treat casualties in the following order:
Unconscious.
Severe bleeding.
Other injuries.

Help the unconscious
- ❏ **Clear airway**
  - If crash victim is alive but not breathing, clear airway. Use your fingers. Quickly remove vomit, loose teeth etc from mouth. Wear rubber gloves if available.
  - Place one hand on the casualty's forehead and the other under the chin.
  - Lift jaw forwards. (Place thumb in victim's mouth for a firmer grip on jaw.) This lifts the tongue clear and unblocks airway.
  - If still not breathing, begin rescue breathing (see above).

- ❏ **Unconscious position**
  - If breathing is regular, place casualty on side in recovery position with upper leg bent at hip and knee. Check the casualty's head remains lifted.
  - Never use pillows or clothing under victim's head.
  - Check victim's breathing often.

- ❏ **Treatment in car**
  - Check airway first. Hold head back. Never leave victim slumped over.
  - If breathing has stopped, begin rescue breathing immediately (see above).
  - Stay with unconscious victims.
  - If vomiting seems likely place victim in semi-prone position on car seat.

- ❏ **Treat bleeding**
  - If wound is to leg, head or arm raise it up while treating (unless fractured). Treat stomach, leg or back wounds while casualty is lying down. For chest wounds, place casualty in a half sitting position, leaning towards injured side.
  - Apply direct pressure over wound.
  - Use clean pad, cloth, handkerchief or victim's hand.
  - Keep pressure on wound until bleeding stops. **Do not use a tourniquet.**

- ❏ **Clear loose debris**
  - Wipe away loose material around wound. Do not touch wound.
  - Do not remove any object embedded in wound. **Never** pull an object out of a puncture wound.

- ❏ **Secure pressure on wound**
  - Wrap bandages around wound. Firm but not tight.

- ❏ **Fracture first aid**
  - Immobilise suspected fractures only if medical assistance will be delayed. Otherwise support them in a comfortable position.
  - Handle carefully to avoid severe pain and shock.
  - If immobilisation is necessary, use belts, ties etc.
  - Use sling for forearm fracture.
  - Bind arm to chest for upper arm fracture.
  - For leg fracture, bandage to good leg above and below fracture. Place padding between knees and ankles.

8 Reassure the casualty

- ❏ Keep casualty warm and comfortable.
- ❏ Tell casualty the ambulance is on its way.

9 Wait for help

- ❏ Keep victim breathing.
- ❏ Do not give anything by mouth.
- ❏ Keep crowds away.

Traveller Information

Banking
Trading banks are open Monday to Friday (except public holidays) between 9.30 am and 4.30 pm. Automatic teller machines are widespread. EFTPOS is available at many outlets. All international credit cards are accepted in New Zealand. Travellers' cheques may be changed at trading banks, Thomas Cook Foreign Exchange offices, hotels, and large stores in the main cities and tourist areas.

Business hours
New Zealand businesses generally operate Monday to Friday between 8.30am and 5pm, though some tourist agencies and airlines have longer hours. Stores usually open 9am to 5.30pm Monday to Friday, with late shopping until 8.30 or 9pm on one or two nights each week (usually Thursday or Friday). Small retailers may be open later, as are petrol stations. Saturday shopping varies; many shops shut at 12.30 or 1pm on a Saturday, but others stay open all afternoon. Many supermarkets and grocery stores, some large chains, most shopping malls and weekend markets are open on Sundays. Convenience stores known as dairies are open 7am to 10pm seven days a week.

Electricity supply
New Zealand's AC electricity supply operates at 230/240 volts, 50 hertz, the same as Australia. Most hotels and motels also provide 110 volt 20 watt AC sockets for electric razors. An adaptor is necessary to operate all other electrical equipment.

Emergencies
In emergencies, dial 111 to summon police, fire or ambulance services.

Telephone services
Most Telecom-provided public telephones are now operated by credit-card-sized cards, available from bookstores, newsagents, tobacconists, petrol stations and some other retail outlets. Some coin-operated telephones remain and there are also some credit card telephones. Local calls from residential telephones are free.

Area codes and international calling codes are in the front of the telephone book, as are international calling charges and instructions.

Health services
Public and private health facilities have a high standard of treatment and care. Doctors and other medical services are listed in the front of the telephone directory.

Visitors are covered by New Zealand's Accident Compensation and Rehabilitation Insurance scheme for personal injury by accident, and are entitled to make a claim irrespective of fault. Benefits include some medical and hospital expenses and physical disability compensation. Medical services other than those necessitated by an accident are not free, and ACC does not cover medical treatment that relates to illness.

Pharmaceuticals and medicines
A 'chemist' is a pharmacist or druggist. Their shops will be open during shopping hours; most cities have urgent after-hours dispensaries, listed in the front of the telephone book under Hospitals. Visitors planning to bring quantities of pharmaceuticals into New Zealand should have a certificate to avoid difficulties with customs.

Postal services
Besides specialist Post Shops in most areas, stamps can be bought from supermarkets, bookstores and grocery shops.

Tipping and service charges
Gratuities are not expected, but if the visitor wishes to leave a tip in gratitude for outstanding service, this is acceptable. Service charges are not added to hotel or restaurant accounts.

Water supply
Tap (faucet) water in New Zealand is fresh, treated and safe to drink. City water supplies are chlorinated and most are fluoridated. The parasite giardia is found in some back-country rivers and lakes. To prevent any problems, ensure water is boiled or otherwise treated before drinking.

Air services
There are three main domestic airlines, Air New Zealand, Ansett New Zealand and Mount Cook Airlines. Numerous commuter airlines service outlying areas.

Rail services
Rail travel in New Zealand is spectacular. The routes pass rugged coastlines, raging rivers, huge ravines, volcanoes, native forests and broad alpine vistas.

Interisland ferry services
Modern ferries crossing Cook Strait link Wellington in the North Island and Picton (Marlborough) in the South Island. The Interislander service carries passengers and vehicles. The new Lynx catamaran is one of the fastest passenger and car carriers in the world.

Bus and coach services
The Magic Bus and InterCity networks, Mount Cook Landlines and Newmans Coach Services together connect most towns in the country. InterCity buses have the widest range of destinations. All offer limited time, unlimited travel passes.

Rental cars
Rental car companies operate in all major cities and resorts. On a couple of the more isolated roads, where special driving conditions create greater risk of damage to the vehicle, rental cars are not insured; check when you rent. Visitors should note that many rental cars in New Zealand are manual (stick-shift) rather than automatic. The minimum hiring age is 21 years.

Driving
Drivers must have a current New Zealand or approved overseas licence. Vehicles drive on the left-hand side of the road. In the rural areas you will often encounter a flock of sheep or a herd of cows. Drive very slowly indeed. Take extra care on the few sections of highway which are not sealed but have a gravel surface.

Campervans
Rented campervans include all kitchen utensils, bedding and linen. You are not limited to camp grounds with this mode of transport. Most camp grounds will allow you to use their dump stations.

Taxis
Taxis owned by a number of companies and independent operators run from stands or on call by telephone 24 hours a day in urban areas. It is easier to telephone for one than to hail one, though in large cities taxi ranks do exist.

Cycle touring
Mid-October to April are the best months for cycling, but if well equipped the rest of the year is no problem. Many resorts hire mountain bikes. Some trains and most buses do not permit bicycles to be taken on board. Helmets are compulsory.

Hitchhiking
Safer in New Zealand than in many countries, but still with its element of risk. As in any other country, women are advised not to hitchhike alone.

Travelpool
This firm, in central Auckland, links travellers going the same way, to share costs and the enjoyment of the ride without the risks associated with hitchhiking.

History

Maori history

Maori history is based on oral tradition. The arrival of the first settlers from their Polynesian homeland of Hawaiki about 1000 years ago has been celebrated in myth and legend. They came in great ocean-going sailing canoes, over a period of many years, and the present-day tribes still trace their origins to the various canoes. The country was named Aotearoa, Land of the Long White Cloud. The people adapted well to the cooler climate, and developed a culture of fishing, hunting and gathering, supplemented by some settled agriculture.

European explorers

The first European to sight New Zealand was the Dutchman Abel Janszoon Tasman, in 1642. He did not land, settling for charting part of the coast.

The British navigational genius Captain James Cook was later commissioned to follow up on Tasman's discovery. On the first of three voyages, in 1769, he landed, first on the east coast of the North Island and later in numerous other places. He traded with the Maori for supplies, circumnavigated both main islands and mapped them with remarkable accuracy. Other early explorers were French (de Surville, du Fresne, D'Entrecasteaux), English (Vancouver) and Italian (Malaspina, who led a Spanish expedition).

Whalers, sealers and missionaries

Once the existence of the country was known, and settlements established in Australia which could be used as a base, it was only a short time before sealers and whalers, mostly British and American, came to hunt the marine mammals.

Kororareka, now known as Russell, was an early centre of activity. Missionaries and traders followed the whalers and sealers in the early 19th century, and pressure began to mount for the British Government to extend colonial status and the rule of law to the area. The missionaries found mixed receptions from the Maori tribes; but they were often among the few Europeans working in the interests of the Maori people as they saw them. They also transcribed the Maori language and recorded much traditional lore.

The Treaty of Waitangi

The controversial Treaty of Waitangi marked the British Government's assumption of sovereignty over New Zealand and was intended to regulate relations between Maori and Pakeha (Europeans). It was initially signed on 6 February 1840, at Waitangi, by Lieutenant-Governor Hobson and a number of Maori chiefs, who did not represent all the tribes. It was never a binding agreement in international law, but it is widely regarded as a foundation of New Zealand constitutional law. It claims to guarantee the Maori possession in perpetuity of their lands, forests and fisheries and to grant them the rights and privileges of British citizens.

European settlers and war

Once some form of British rule had been imposed on the country, ambitious men in Britain began to plan settlement schemes. The Free Church of Scotland sent a group to found Dunedin, while the New Zealand Company founded Wellington, Nelson and Christchurch. At this time began the problems of land ownership which have plagued New Zealand ever since and led to its only internal wars. Maori concepts of land ownership were tribally rather than individually based, and the early settlers would often 'buy' land (usually for less than its worth) from an individual Maori who did not have the exclusive right to it.

During the 1860s, the North Island was torn by armed conflict over these and other problems including Maori self-determination. Although the European armies were victorious, the Maori displayed impressive military ability in strategy, tactics and fortification, and relentless courage.

After the wars, much land was confiscated, including some belonging to tribes which had been neutral or even friendly in the conflict.

Gold, wool and government innovations

From the 1860s to the 1880s, gold drew many to Otago, Westland and the Coromandel, and large herds of sheep began to be established on cleared land.

In the late 19th century, New Zealand became the 'social laboratory of the world', being the first sovereign state to introduce votes for women (1893) and an old age pension (1898), as well as a free public health service, minimum wage structures and independent industrial arbitration between employees and employers.

The twentieth century

Named as an autonomous dominion in 1907 (there had been responsible elected government since 1854), New Zealand still felt close ties to Britain, which was regarded as 'home' by many New Zealand-born people. In World War I, 42% of the male population served in the armed forces.

Many New Zealand servicemen fought overseas in World War II and the country also hosted a large number of Americans on their way to the war in the Pacific. Since then, Britain has turned to the European Community rather than to the British Commonwealth of its former colonies for trade, and most New Zealanders of British descent no longer feel as much affinity with the country of their ancestors as their parents or grandparents did. As links with Britain have lessened, links with the USA and the Pacific Rim have increased.

Since World War II, advances in transport and communications have reduced New Zealand's isolation from the rest of the world, and New Zealanders have become prominent in a number of fields internationally, notably sport and the arts.

Fotopacific – J. Speller

THE TREATY OF WAITANGI was signed on the front lawn of the Treaty House, Waitangi.

Climate & Statistics

The seasons are the reverse of the Northern Hemisphere: summer December to February, autumn March to May, winter June to August, spring September to November. Because the winters are relatively mild, however, spring growth often starts to appear in late August. The temperature change from north to south is also the reverse of the Northern Hemisphere; average temperatures at sea level range from 16°C in the subtropical north to about 10°C in the temperate south. High temperatures, occasionally over 30°C, occur on the east coasts of both islands during summer, and temperatures over 40°C have been recorded in Marlborough and Canterbury. The coldest winters occur in Central Otago, where an extreme minimum temperature of −21°C has been recorded.

A particularly unpolluted atmosphere, and the hole in the ozone layer over the Antarctic, mean that protection from the sun's ultraviolet rays in the form of sunscreen preparations, hats and sunglasses is necessary in summer and on the ski slopes. Even on an overcast day, ultraviolet radiation penetrates the clouds. When you are outside during the summer months remember that it takes only 10 to 20 minutes to get a painful burn. An hour in the midday sun can cause blisters and peeling for days after. Over a period of years sunburn can lead to melanoma and other skin cancers.

Location	Rainfall		Sunshine	Temperature					
	Annual		Annual	Daily maximum		Daily minimum		Extremes	
				Jan	Jul	Jan	Jul	highest	lowest
	mm	days	hours	°C	°C	°C	°C	°C	°C
Kaitaia	1318	135	2067	23.9	15.4	15.6	8.5	30.6	-0.9
Kerikeri	1724	135	1992	24.4	15.8	14.0	6.6	34.3	-2.0
Auckland	1106	121	2071	22.8	14.2	16.6	8.2	32.4	-0.1
Tauranga	1225	109	2225	23.7	14.2	14.4	4.9	33.7	-5.3
Rotorua	1444	117	2105	22.9	12.0	12.6	3.0	35.2	-6.9
Taupo	1123	116	1987	23.3	11.1	11.4	2.1	33.0	-6.3
Hamilton	1182	127	2027	23.8	13.5	12.6	3.6	34.7	-9.9
Waiouru	1075	141	1770*	19.1	7.3	8.2	0.1	29.3	-9.2
Gisborne	1041	110	2186	24.8	14.0	13.5	4.5	38.1	-3.4
Napier	814	93	2185	24.5	13.8	14.5	4.2	36.9	-6.5
New Plymouth	1456	138	2175	21.7	13.1	13.4	5.4	30.4	-2.4
Wanganui	870	114	2051	22.3	12.9	14.0	5.3	32.3	-2.3
Palmerston North	959	120	1723	22.3	12.2	13.3	4.4	33.0	-6.9
Wellington	1269	124	2024	20.3	11.2	13.4	5.9	31.1	-1.9
Westport	2218	168	1824	20.0	12.4	12.4	4.5	28.6	-3.5
Hokitika	2807	169	1837	19.3	11.8	11.6	2.7	29.7	-3.2
Milford Sound	6589	183	1780*	18.7	9.1	10.4	1.4	28.3	-5.0
Nelson	976	94	2371	22.2	12.0	12.9	1.3	36.3	-6.6
Blenheim	648	75	2472	23.9	12.8	12.7	2.1	36.0	-8.8
Hanmer Forest	1165	117	1810	22.8	9.5	8.9	-1.5	37.1	-13.2
Christchurch	645	86	2066	22.6	11.1	12.3	1.6	41.6	-7.2
Timaru	551	77	1906	20.9	10.6	12.1	1.5	39.8	-8.9
Lake Tekapo	610	78	2227	21.3	6.0	9.0	-2.5	33.3	-15.6
Alexandra	358	69	1994	25.0	8.4	10.9	-1.8	37.2	-11.7
Queenstown	864	98	1885	22.2	8.0	10.5	0.0	34.1	-9.0
Dunedin	799	124	1595	18.9	9.9	11.4	3.1	35.7	-8.0
Invercargill	1087	157	1580	18.5	9.5	9.4	1.1	32.2	-7.4

* Estimates
Averages based on the 1965-94 period

The land

Highest mountains
(height in m)

Cook	3754
Tasman	3500
Dampier	3440
Silberhorn	3279
Lendenfeldt	3201
Ruapehu	2797

Longest rivers
(length in km)

Waikato	425
Clutha	322
Wanganui	290
Taieri	288

Largest lakes
(area in km²)

Taupo	606
Te Anau	344
Wakatipu	293
Wanaka	192
Ellesmere	181

The people

Total population is approximately 3,540,000 (September 1994). Around 85% of the population live in urban areas; largest urban areas:

Auckland	929,300
Wellington	329,000
Christchurch	318,100
Hamilton	158,300
Dunedin	112,400

Almost 75% of the population live in the North Island (2.64 million).

Ethnic origin

European	79.5%
New Zealand Maori	13%
Pacific Islands	5%

Other important minorities include Chinese (1.3%), Indian (0.9%)

Trade

(values in $NZ millions)

Principal Exports (1994)

meat	2799
lamb and mutton	1247
beef and veal	1317
dairy produce	2795
milk, cream, yoghurt	1342
butter	791
cheese	582
forest products	2470
fruit and vegetables	1068
wool	1180
fish	1074
hides, skins and leather	676
aluminium and aluminium items	742
casein and caseinates	575
mineral fuels	409
electrical and mechanical machinery	1324

Principal Imports (1994)

machinery and mechanical appliances	3018
electrical equipment	1865
motor vehicles	2260
crude petroleum	728
plastics	825
optical, photographic, technical and surgical equipment	618
iron and steel and articles of iron and steel	610
aircraft	743

Conversion factors
New Zealand has used the metric system since 1975. Measurements used in this book:

1m (metre) = 1.1 yards; 1km (kilometre) = 0.62 miles; 1ha (hectare) = 2.5 acres.

To convert °C to °F: multiply by 9, divide by 5, add 32

Land & Sea

New Zealand is sometimes called 'the world's biggest farm', with an economy strongly based on agriculture and horticulture (60% of export earnings and 20% of gross domestic product come from these industries). In recent years, with world demand for agricultural products falling or being met from other sources, New Zealand has begun to seek diversification, but meat, dairy products and wool remain among its major overseas export earners. Because of this, agricultural and quarantine regulations are strict, and agricultural inspectors will fumigate any organic material which comes into the country to prevent the importation of pests and diseases.

Agricultural research is advanced, and selective breeding has been developed to a high degree. Grasslands management has enabled the rugged terrain to support high stock numbers, and part of this has been New Zealand's pioneering of aerial agricultural fertilisation of the soil and sowing of seed. Even rainfall and plentiful sunlight means that pasture grasses grow well for eight to 12 months of the year, and in the mild climate the livestock is able to live outside throughout the year and feed almost entirely on grass. This makes for better meat flavour and cheaper management. Rotational grazing is often managed with the help of electric fencing.

Farmstays offer a wonderful opportunity to gain an insight into one of the world's most agriculturally advanced nations.

Dairy farming

Dairying is mainly a North Island industry (with 90% of the dairy cattle in New Zealand in the North Island). Over 14,000 dairy herds, totalling 3.5 million cattle, are farmed in New Zealand. Most are owner-operated, though about 3000 employ 'sharemilkers' who provide labour in exchange for a share in the profits. Herds are large, averaging 140 milking cows (since on the best land 3.5 cows per hectare can be carried), and mechanical milking was pioneered in New Zealand to cope with this; some automated sheds can milk more than 350 cows in an hour. Milk is then cooled and pumped to vats from which road tankers collect it once or twice daily.

About 330,000 tonnes of milk fat result annually, around 13% being consumed as milk or fed to stock (including beef calves and pigs). The rest is used for the dairy products, casein and caseinates of which New Zealand is the world's largest exporter. These include milk powders (skim milk, wholemilk, and buttermilk powder), cream products (butter, anhydrous milk fat and ghee), and cheeses, mainly cheddar but with a growing number of French-style speciality cheeses. All these products together provide 20% of New Zealand's export income.

Except for a small volume manufactured by 'boutique' cheese makers, all of the 800,000 tonnes of dairy products made in New Zealand each year is manufactured by the 18 cooperative dairy companies, which are owned by farmers in proportion to the milk supplied by each and controlled by a board elected from among the suppliers. Dairy companies also elect directors to the New Zealand Dairy Board. The farmers hence control the processing and marketing structures of the industry, which receives no government subsidies or other assistance.

The dairy companies are usually large multiproduct manufacturers, some operating several sites. Sophisticated processing technology allows flexibility in product lines according to the greatest profitability at the time.

Research and development produces new products, targets them to specific markets, and modifies existing products to meet similarly specialised markets. The New Zealand Dairy Research Institute is one of the world's most advanced organisations in this field, and is based near Palmerston North. It is financed primarily through the Dairy Board and secondarily by the government's Foundation for Research, Science and Technology.

Cheesemaking is an art and a science, producing a versatile food which New Zealand has been exporting since the 1840s. Cheddar is, as it always has been, the most favoured variety, but many others are now manufactured. More than 60 varieties, including those unique to New Zealand as well as high-quality versions of European cheeses, are produced. Most cheeses are made from cows' milk, with some goats' or ewes' milk cheese.

Meat farming

New Zealand has a modern, dynamic, competitive and innovative export meat industry, which employs tens of thousands of people – farmers, farm workers, meat processing workers and those in servicing roles – and earns nearly $NZ2.8 billion

ORCHARDS outside Motueka, Nelson.

Focus NZ – R. Fowler

Land & Sea

HARVESTING farmed mussels, Marlborough.

Stephen Robinson

Beef farming

Beef cattle numbers have been slowly increasing in recent years and there are now about 5 million beef cattle in New Zealand. Two-thirds of the beef exported is high-specification manufacturing quality aimed at North American food processors. Premium steer cuts go to the Caribbean, Middle East, Asia and the Pacific Basin. South Korea has become a major importer of New Zealand beef, and the Japanese market is also expected to grow.

Other animals

Goats and deer have been developed as commercial animals over the past few years. Deer are farmed for venison and velvet, and goats for milk, meat or weed control as well as for mohair, cashmere or cashgora (the main use). Pigs are farmed for domestic consumption only, and in fact small amounts of pig meat are imported.

annually in overseas export, making it the top export earner among the country's industries. The industry began with the first refrigerated ships in 1882.

Most of New Zealand's meat goes overseas, and hides, skins and other related products add significantly to the earnings from beef, lamb and mutton. By-products of the meat industry include slipe wool for carpets and garments, tallow for soaps, tyres, shoes and detergents, sausage casings, blood anticoagulants, and pharmaceuticals.

Although New Zealand supplies a sixth of the meat traded in the world, it produces only 1% of the world's total meat production. Most countries consume 95% of the meat they produce, but New Zealand consumes only 25% and exports the remainder.

Sheep farming

The best-known New Zealand statistic is the ratio of sheep to people: 20 to one at the height of the season. There are about 24,000 farms in New Zealand which stock mainly sheep, occupying over 11 million hectares which together support 60 million sheep, in flocks averaging about 1800. Depending on the quality of the land, one to 25 sheep can be run per hectare.

Most of the wool-producing farms are found in the hill country of the North Island, but sheep are found almost everywhere, especially in the dryer eastern hills of both islands. The country is now known as a quality source of both meat and wool from sheep. Much of the fine meat comes from

the more than 40 million lambs born each year, about 60% of which are exported, with most of the balance retained as breeding stock. Lambs are also an important wool source.

New Zealand wool is noted for length and colour, relative absence of vegetable matter and high yield. The wools are coarse and strong compared to the finer Merino wool of Australia and South Africa, but yield about 75% clean wool, compared to 50-60% in other countries.

Most wool is shorn from live sheep, in some places twice a year. Shearing is a skilled job, done on the farm site either by a shearing contractor or by the farmer and his family. A unique New Zealand shearing style, emphasising economy of effort, has been developed and is imitated throughout the world.

A wide variety of sheep breeds, scientific farm management practices, and the climate and geography of the country all contribute to the highest quality of sheep meat and wool. New Zealand is the world's second largest wool producer on a scoured (clean-washed) basis, and wool is the country's fourth largest export earner. If meat is counted, sheep constitute the largest New Zealand export industry.

Over 80% of the raw and processed wools produced in New Zealand are exported, bringing in over NZ$1 billion in the 1991/92 year from more than 50 countries. New Zealanders are also the second largest users of wool per capita in the world.

Orcharding

In many parts of the country, long windbreaks and signs offering surplus fruit at roadside stalls mark orchard country. The long, mild autumns and microclimates caused by the hilly country and general closeness to the sea mean that much fruit can be produced. In some areas (mainly Northland and the Bay of Plenty), frost-free conditions allow subtropical fruits such as avocados, feijoas, kiwifruit, tamarillos and passionfruit to flourish, while others (Auckland, Waikato, Hawke's Bay, Marlborough, Nelson, Canterbury, Otago and Southland) have the consistent frosts necessary to set fruit in apricots, peaches, plums, nectarines, cherries and berryfruits (blackcurrants, boysenberries, raspberries and strawberries). Citrus is grown commercially mainly in Northland and the Bay of Plenty. Apples and pears for export are grown mainly in the Hawke's Bay and Nelson.

The most famous New Zealand fruit is the kiwifruit, a fuzzy brown berry with tangy green flesh containing high amounts of vitamin C. Originally from China, it was developed as a commercial crop in the eastern North Island.

Crop farming

Arable crops are used mainly for animal feeds, but malting barley is used for the manufacture of beer, and also exported. Most other crops, including beans, peas, carrots, potatoes and sweet corn, go for domestic consumption, although large quantities of onions are exported, most

Land & Sea

TIMBER PROCESSING PLANT, Nelson.

Stephen Robinson

notably from the Pukekohe area, south of Auckland.

Apiculture

A specialist product popular internationally, New Zealand honey is mainly produced from clover, though native honey sources are also used. Bees are also used for crop pollination. New Zealand mead (brewed from honey) is enjoyed particularly in Japan.

Winemaking

Begun by European immigrants, notably Croatians who came to dig kauri gum, the New Zealand wine industry has been greatly improved over recent years by 'Kiwi ingenuity' in adapting existing agricultural and industrial methods to this new purpose. New Zealand varietal table wines are now increasingly prominent in international competition, and win top awards against the best wines of Europe, California and Australia, making New Zealand one of the world's top ten wine producers.

As a cool climate country, well provided with water and with a long autumn during which the grapes can ripen slowly to a full flavour, New Zealand is ideal for wine-making, and a constantly rising standard is evident among its winemakers. The number of wineries and the volume of wine produced increases every year, and the 1995 harvest produced 74,500 tonnes of grapes.

Notable New Zealand wines are generally those known for their distinct taste profiles and intense flavour, such as whites Sauvignon Blanc, Chardonnay, Riesling, Muller Thurgau and Gewurztztraminer, and reds Cabernet Sauvignon and Pinot Noir. Some good Méthode Champenoise and sweet white dessert wines are also being produced.

The main wine growing areas are Auckland, Gisborne, Hawke's Bay, Wairarapa, Nelson, Marlborough, Canterbury and Central Otago.

Fishing

New Zealand has one of the world's largest Exclusive Economic Zones, set at 200 miles from the coast and enclosing an area of about 1.2 million square nautical miles, within which all fishing rights are reserved. Of about 1000 fish species in these waters some 10% are fished commercially. Much of the area is too deep for bottom fishing, so despite the large fishing zone, New Zealand is not one of the world's richest fishing nations. However, the fishing industry is still a major export earner for the country.

An annual quota system is used to manage the fisheries resources, ensuring that such popular species as tarakihi, snapper and trevally are not fished out. There are five main areas of the seafood industry: inshore, deepwater, pelagic, shellfish and aquaculture. There are about 30 inshore species including flounder, sole, snapper, john dory, groper, bluenose, tarakihi, blue cod and monkfish. The deepwater fishes include hoki, hake, orange roughy and oreo dory. The pelagic (midwater) species include tuna, kahawai, jack mackerel and shark, and the shellfish include coldwater lobster (crayfish), squid, scallops, paua, scampi and oysters. Salmon and green-lipped mussels are farmed.

Forestry

Some of the world's largest plantation forests are found here, growing exotic timber for use in pulp and paper mills and for lumber. Around 1.2 million of the 7.4 million hectares of forest in New Zealand is exotic plantation, and these are now reaching a stage of large-scale use. Radiata pine, introduced from California, is a fast-growing species that has been improved genetically in forestry labs. It accounts for about 90% of New Zealand's plantation forests.

Forestry companies separate the wood into grades depending on its suitability for particular end-uses. Those parts that are not of lumber quality are converted into newsprint for sale to around 20 countries around the Pacific, and into surplus chemical pulp, which is also exported. Wood-based panels are another end-use, with fibreboard, particle board, hardboard and plywood all being produced for use in residential and commercial construction and high-quality furniture. A range of tissues, lightweight papers and other specialist papers and boards for the domestic market are also produced.

Native forests are now protected from logging for purposes of planting exotics, and the concentration is on the existing forests as a sustainable and renewable resource. Most State forests are managed by the Department of Conservation. Almost a quarter of New Zealand's land area is covered by natural forest. The sale of many State exotic forests in 1990 means that around three-quarters of the nation's forest resources are now privately owned, although the sale covered only management and cutting rights, and not the land.

National, Forest & Maritime Parks

New Zealand's first national park, Tongariro, was gifted to the people of New Zealand in 1887 by the paramount chief of the Ngati Tuwharetoa, Te Heuheu Tukino IV. It was the second national park to be set aside anywhere in the world. There are now 13 national parks throughout the country, supplemented by 19 forest parks with a lesser protected status, three maritime parks, and nearly 4000 regional parks and reserves of various sizes.

National parks

Te Urewera National Park
Area: 212,672ha
A vast, forested wilderness within reach of Rotorua, with a rich heritage of Maori history and legend. The largest untouched stretch of native forest in the North Island. Crystal clear lakes and rivers. Excellent tramping and short walks through luxuriant forest, including the 51km Lake Waikaremoana Track. Birdwatching, hunting, fishing, canoeing, boating.

Egmont National Park
Area: 33,534ha
Centred around the volcanic cone of Mt Taranaki/Egmont, with more than 320km of walks and tracks. Subalpine forest, volcanic landforms, mountain streams and waterfalls, and alpine herbfields. Snow, ice and rock climbing. Panoramic views from the summit. Only 30km from New Plymouth. Note: The mountain weather can be harsh and changeable. Care is needed above the bushline at all times.

Whanganui National Park
Area: 74,231ha
A river park based around the historic Whanganui River, in a rugged setting of dense forest, Maori historic sites and abandoned farm settlements. Accessible by road or jet boat. Excellent long-distance canoeing suitable for novices as well as experienced canoeists, rafting, jet boating. Short walks and longer tramps, including Matemateaonga and Mangapurua tracks. Hunting, guided walks and river trips.

Tongariro National Park
Area: 78,651ha
A spectacular alpine park with active volcanoes Ruapehu, Tongariro and Ngauruhoe. Lava flows, active craters, hot springs lakes, grasslands, forest and alpine herbfields. World Heritage Area. Well-developed facilities enabling year-round walking and tramping, winter skiing, mountain, ice and rock climbing.

Abel Tasman National Park
Area: 22,350ha
A small coastal park within easy reach of Nelson. Its unspoilt golden beaches and forested interior are delightful at any time of the year. A park for people of all ages, with coastal walking and camping, fishing, sailing, kayaking, and inland tracks and caves (experienced cavers only). The Coastal Track, a family walk taking 3-4 days, is very popular in summer.

Kahurangi National Park
Area: 376,572ha
New Zealand's thirteenth national park, designated as such in 1995. A large wilderness park accessible from Nelson or the West Coast, with mountains, rivers, lakes, karst landforms, forest, tussock downlands, alpine herbfields and coastline. Offers some of New Zealand's best tramping, from rugged wilderness routes to well-known tracks, including the Wangapeka, Heaphy, Cobb Valley and Mt Arthur Tablelands. Mountaineering, hunting, fishing, caving, rafting. Tours of the Honeycomb Caves and Oparara Valley, helicopter trips. Road access to the main tracks, but limited public transport.

Nelson Lakes National Park
Area: 96,121ha
A compact alpine park accessible from Nelson or the West Coast, with beech forests, rivers and glacial lakes (Rotoiti and Rotoroa). Year-round scenic walks, tramping, mountaineering, ski mountaineering, ice skating, hunting, fishing, sailing and canoeing.

SMALL LAGOONS on the West Sabine, Nelson Lakes National Park.

Key-Light Image Library Ltd – B. Enting

National, Forest & Maritime Parks

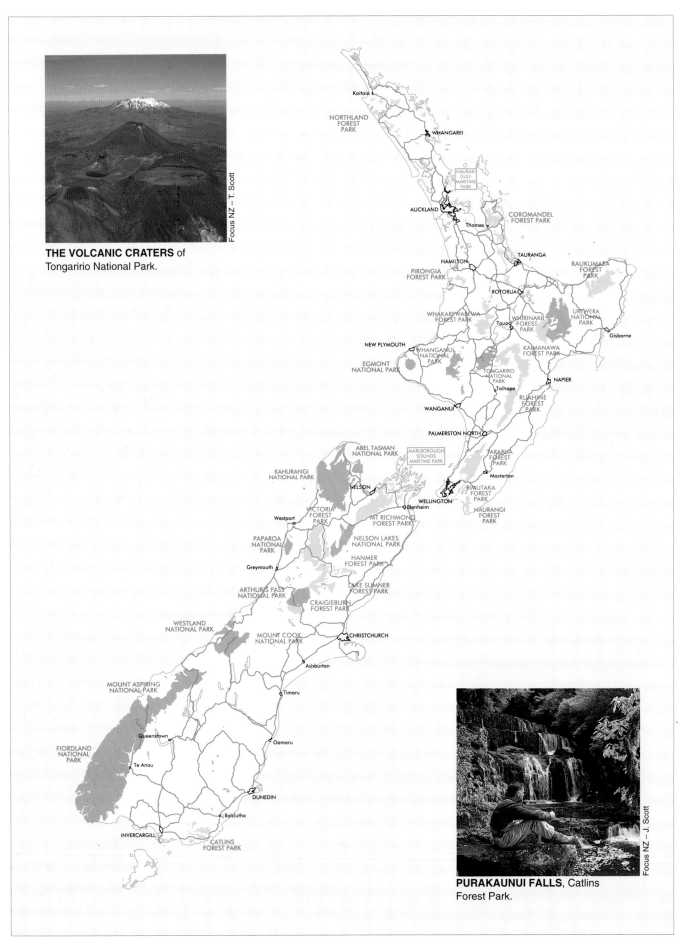

THE VOLCANIC CRATERS of Tongaririo National Park.

Focus NZ – T. Scott

PURAKAUNUI FALLS, Catlins Forest Park.

Focus NZ – J. Scott

National, Forest & Maritime Parks

Key-Light Image Library Ltd – N. Bishop

WINTER SNOW in beech forest at Haast Pass, Mt Aspiring National Park.

Paparoa National Park
Area: 30,327ha
A small, diverse park on the South Island's wild West Coast, with luxuriant coastal forests, limestone canyons, caves, underground streams, as well as a spectacular coastline with the famous 'pancake' rocks and blowholes at Punakaiki. Easily accessible coastal walks and longer tracks, including a pack track from the gold-rush days. Camping, canoeing, rock climbing and caving for experienced cavers.

Arthur's Pass National Park
Area: 99,270ha
In the heart of the Southern Alps, featuring rugged mountains, forests, alpine vegetation and kea (alpine parrot). Tramping, climbing, skiing, hunting, short walks, camping. Scenic highway and railway.

Westland National Park
Area: 117,547ha
Extends from the highest peaks of the Southern Alps to a wild, remote coastline. Glaciers, scenic lakes and dense rainforest. Remains of old gold-mining towns on the coast. Easy access to Franz Josef and Fox Glaciers, forest and coastal walks. Mountaineering, ski touring, hunting and fishing. Guided tours of the glaciers, scenic drives and flights available. World Heritage Area.

Mt Cook National Park
Area: 70,013ha
An alpine park, containing New Zealand's highest mountain and longest glacier. World Heritage Area. A focus for mountaineering and ski touring, but easy family walks and scenic flights also provide spectacular views. Limited scope for tramping and hunting.

Mt Aspiring National Park
Area: 355,518ha
Remote and spectacular alpine wilderness accessible from Wanaka, Queenstown or the Haast Pass, with mountains, glaciers, hanging valleys and lakes. World Heritage Area. Contains the well-known Routeburn and Rees-Dart tracks. Wilderness mountaineering, hunting, fishing, guided walks. Outstanding scenery along the Haast Pass Highway.

Fiordland National Park
Area: 1,252,297ha
A vast remote wilderness, with snow-capped mountains, glacial lakes and valleys, fiords, islands, waterfalls and dense forest. World Heritage Area. Contains some of New Zealand's best-known tramping tracks, including the Milford, Kepler, Dusky, Routeburn and Hollyford. Fishing, hunting, guided walks, cruises on lakes and fiords, scenic flights. Penguins, seals, dolphins, spectacular coastal features. Note: Bookings are essential for the Milford Track.

Special interest parks

Lewis Pass National Reserve
Area: 13,845ha
A landscape of mountain peaks, hot springs, lakes, forest, snow tussock and

19

National, Forest & Maritime Parks

alpine herbfields. There is access from the scenic Lewis Pass Highway to a wide range of tramping and hunting. Also easy walks, fishing, picnicking and roadside camping. Start of the St James Walkway.

Otago Goldfields Park
Area: many small sites scattered across the Otago region
A glimpse of New Zealand's gold-mining heritage. The old mining sites, historic buildings, museums and reconstructed mining settlements are dotted over scenic landscapes, including tussockland and rock tors. Year-round activities include historic walks along old mining trails, gold panning, horse trekking, mountain bike touring, scenic drives and white water rafting.

Forest parks

Northland Forest Park
Area: approx. 80,000ha
Subtropical rainforest dominated by giant kauri, including New Zealand's biggest tree, Tane Mahuta. The park is made up of many separate pockets of forest. Lots of short walks and several longer tracks. You can view the forests from the road. A must for botanists and birdwatchers.

Coromandel Forest Park
Area: approx. 73,000ha
Easily accessible from Auckland, Hamilton or Tauranga, this is a popular recreational park with luxuriant forest, old volcanic landforms, and historic mining and milling sites. Activities include easy walks, fishing, swimming, tramping in the forest and nearby coastal farm parks. Fishing, sailing, swimming and diving around the coast.

Kaimai-Mamaku Forest Park
Area: 37,141ha
A narrow, rugged, forested park running the length of the Kaimai-Mamaku ranges. Within reach of Rotorua, Tauranga, Hamilton and Auckland, it offers scope for bush walks, tramping, picnicking, rock climbing, hunting, and exploring old gold-mining and kauri-milling sites. Public transport available to within 5km of the park.

Pirongia Forest Park
Area: 16,738ha
Small and densely forested, with interesting plant life, this park is centred around the slopes of three extinct volcanoes. Only 30km from Hamilton. Ideal for short walks and 1 or 2-day tramps. Hunting.

Raukumara Forest Park
Area: 115,000ha
Rugged forested ranges, featuring one of New Zealand's foremost wild and scenic rivers, the Motu. Access is difficult, but it is well worth the effort for those who want to get off the beaten track. White water rafting, wilderness tramping, hunting.

Pureora Forest Park
Area: 72,335ha
Magnificent, dense, podocarp forest with rich bird life, on the western side of Lake Taupo. Home of the rare North Island kokako. Forest viewing tower. Forest walks, camping, birdwatching, scenic drives, tramping, hunting.

Whirinaki Forest Park
Area: 60,900ha
Famous for its magnificent podocarp forests. Short and day walks and tramping, as well as fishing and canoeing on the Whirinaki River. About 100km from Rotorua.

Kaweka Forest Park
Area: 67,145ha
A back-country park offering good rafting, canoeing, hunting, fishing, and a range of tramping for experienced trampers and day walkers. Picnic and camping spots at road ends.

Kaimanawa Forest Park
Area: 76,348ha
A remote, rugged mountain wilderness, accessible from Turangi. Plenty of scope for hunting, wilderness tramping, fishing, rafting and canoeing.

Ruahine Forest Park
Area: 93,068ha
Rugged ranges with a network of tramping tracks through forest, river systems, tussock and open tops. Hunting, riverside camping. Accessible from Palmerston North or Napier.

Rimutaka Forest Park
Area: 19,670ha
Popular recreational park only 45km from Wellington city, with walks and tracks to suit everyone, including the Rimutaka Incline Walk, following an historic rail link. Turakirae Head Scientific Reserve and seal colony are found nearby on the coast. Camping and picnicking are both possible.

Haurangi Forest Park
Area: 19,373ha
Remote forested and scrub-covered ranges suitable for hunters and experienced trampers with their own transport. Spectacular coastline and seal colony near Cape Palliser. Coastal camping and fishing, and several short walks, including one to an unusual rock formation, the Putangirua Pinnacles.

Tararua Forest Park
Area: 116,627ha
Within easy reach of Wellington and Palmerston North. The rugged forested interior offers a wide variety of overnight tramping. Plenty of short walks, picnic and camping spots near the edges of the park. Note: The weather on the tops can be severe. Be well prepared at all times of the year.

MILFORD SOUND and Mitre Peak, Fiordland National Park.

Key-Light Image Library Ltd – G. Mason

National, Forest & Maritime Parks

Key-Light Image Library Ltd – B. Enting

WATERFALL, Waipoua Forest, Northland Forest Park.

Mt Richmond Forest Park
Area: 177,109ha
Rugged and forested, yet only minutes away from Nelson. Over 250km of walks and tracks, some following historic trails. Hunting, fishing, riverside camping and picnicking.

Victoria Forest Park
Area: 209,237ha
Rugged and mountainous, this large park centred on Reefton contains some of New Zealand's finest beech forests and mining relics of the historic Reefton quartz gold fields. Walks along old mining tracks, tramping, climbing, hunting, fishing, gold panning, camping, four-wheel drives and horse trekking.

Hanmer Forest Park
Area: 16,852ha
A thermal holiday resort within easy reach of Christchurch. Activities include easy walks through stands of native and exotic trees, tramping, rafting, jet boating, horse trekking, and swimming in thermal pools at Hanmer Springs.

Lake Sumner Forest Park
Area: 73,968ha
A trampers' park, accessible from Christchurch or the Lewis Pass Highway, with mountains, rivers, lakes, hot springs and beech forests. Contains Harper's Pass, one of the lowest crossings of the Southern Alps. Hunting, fishing, birdwatching are possible.

Craigieburn Forest Park
Area: 44,000ha
A small mountainous park in the scenic Arthur's Pass Highway best known for its winter ski areas. Excellent beech forest. Offers a good range of tramping, short walks, hunting, camping and picnicking.

Catlins Forest Park
Area: 58,131ha
Luxuriant coastal forest 100km from Invercargill and 130km from Dunedin. A variety of walks and tracks lead through the forest and along a rugged coastline of cliffs, bays and sea caves where penguins, seals and Hector's dolphins are often seen. Historic timber-milling sites and ancient petrified forests. Fishing, hunting.

Maritime parks

Bay of Islands Maritime and Historic Park
Natural beauty and historic significance are key features of this subtropical park of islands, bays, beaches, tidal inlets and mangroves. Activities for everyone, including visits to historic and archaeological sites, forest and coastal walks, boating, swimming, diving, big game fishing and camping.

Hauraki Gulf Maritime Park
A huge maritime park with 47 islands right on the doorstep of New Zealand's largest city, Auckland. Plenty of scope for yachting and water sports, and the inner islands are easily accessible for picnicking, camping and walking trips. Highlights include: Rangitoto Island, New Zealand's newest volcano; Tiritiri Matangi Island, an open sanctuary for endangered species; Kawau Island, with its historic Mansion House; and North Head, an area steeped in military history. Outer islands are mainly nature reserves closed to casual visitors. Great Barrier Island, a large, partly forested island on the edge of the park, has opportunities for camping and a range of walks and tramps.

Focus NZ – B. Moorhead

KAWAU ISLAND, Hauraki Gulf Maritime Park.

Marlborough Sounds Maritime Park
One of New Zealand's most popular summer holiday places, featuring drowned river valleys, islands, sheltered inlets and sea. Fishing, boating, scenic cruises, sea kayaking, coastal camping, scenic and historic walks, tramping. Launch transport for fishing, sightseeing and tramping trips. Scenic drive around Queen Charlotte Sound.

Walking & Tramping

Tramping, known in other English-speaking countries as hiking, trekking or bushwalking, is one of the most popular and certainly one of the cheapest outdoor activities in New Zealand. It can range from an easy, brief walk to several days in 'the bush,' as the often breathtaking native forest is known. The landscape is rugged and at least hilly, if not mountainous, over most of the country, and tramping often involves hill climbs.

No excursion into the New Zealand bush should be undertaken without warm, preferably woollen or polypropylene clothes, raingear, sturdy footwear, plenty of food and a good topographical map. The Department of Conservation (DOC) or a sports store will tell you what you need. For overnight or longer tramps a tent and camping stove may be necessary.

Visitor centres close to tracks and huts provide intention books, which should be filled in with such details as names of each member of the party and how long each intends to tramp. All hut tickets should be bought before embarking on your tramp.

To help you plan and enjoy your visit to New Zealand's parks DOC provides:

- Visitor centres with displays and information about each park.
- Huts, walking tracks, campsites, picnic spots and other facilities.
- Facilities for less mobile people.
- Advice on routes, weather, equipment and safety in the outdoors.
- Maps, handbooks and souvenirs, on sale at DOC offices and visitor centres.

Access

Parks and protected areas are open all year round and can be visited without a permit. There is no charge to go into the parks, or to use basic facilities such as visitor centres, tracks, toilets or picnic places. A charge is made for some brochures and to stay overnight in most huts (hut tickets or passes must be bought before the trip; details from DOC).

Commercial sightseeing, adventure or education tours, transport and accommodation are options in many parks. Permits or licences are needed for hunting and fishing. Dogs are not allowed in national parks, but may be allowed into other parks with a permit. Inquire at a DOC office near the park.

Look after yourself

Although New Zealand has a mild climate the weather can change quickly at any time of the year. Heavy rain, snow and gales can hit mountain ranges even in the summer. This means trips into the outdoors are always potentially hazardous.

Talk to park staff or read information guides before setting off into the bush or mountains, and take a topographical map, high-energy foods, warm clothing and wet-weather gear. Make sure someone knows your plans (remember to let them know once you return). Leave details in intention books at the visitor centre and in huts.

If you need to take drinking water from rivers or other natural sources it is best to boil, chemically treat or filter it before drinking.

Accommodation

There are around 1000 backcountry huts provided by tramping clubs or DOC. These are sited about five hours' walk apart; on popular tracks, they may be full by the time you reach them, and it is necessary to carry a tent. They are usually equipped with basic bunks, and may contain cooking facilities, though not utensils. Hut charges vary from $4 to $20 per night.

Many guiding companies maintain lodges on the more popular tracks, for the exclusive use of their customers. These are rather more luxurious than the huts and provide supplies of food, meaning that trampers only have to carry a small pack between them. Most guided walks run for four to five days and cost from just over $500 to around $1000 per person.

NIKAU PALMS by the beach, Heaphy Track.

Key-Light Image Library Ltd – N. Bishop

Walking & Tramping

Walkways

Walkways, walking tracks in rural and urban areas, often cross private land and are an alternative to back-country tracks through forested areas. They vary from a half-hour wander to four or five days for the St James Walkway. Possibly unique in the world is Auckland's Coast to Coast Walkway, which takes around four hours.

Ninety Mile Beach
Te Paki to south end of Ninety Mile Beach
103km, 22 hours
(easy)
Part of the New Zealand Walkway System, from scenic Cape Reinga and south along the country's longest beach.

Lake Waikaremoana
Round the lake from Onepoto
43km, 3-5 days
(easy to medium)
One of the most popular North Island tramps, going most of the way around the beautiful lake in Te Urewera National Park. There are spectacular views of the ranges, fine beaches and great trout fishing.

Abel Tasman Coastal Track
Along coast of Abel Tasman National Park
3-4 days
(easy)
One of the most beautiful coastal walks in the world; also the most popular in New Zealand. Beaches, bays and tidal areas unmatched anywhere else.

Heaphy Track
Collingwood to Karamea
76km, 4-6 days
(easy to medium)
A popular walk through Kahurangi National Park to the wild and rocky West Coast, with a wide range of scenery.

Routeburn Track
Lake Wakatipu to Upper Hollyford Valley
3-4 days
(medium)
An alpine track leading through Mt Aspiring and Fiordland National Parks, taking in rainforest, subalpine scrub and spectacular vistas. Very popular and heavily used.

Hollyford Track
Hollyford Valley to Martins Bay
4-5 days
(medium)
Through the thick rainforest of Fiordland National Park, with fine trout fishing, mountain scenery and colonies of seals and penguins at the coast.

BRAIDED RIVER on the Milford Track.

John Blackwell

Milford Track
Lake Te Anau to Milford Sound
53km, 3-5 days
(medium)
New Zealand's best-known track, so popular that it is necessary to book some time in advance before walking it. Rainforest, alpine meadows and dramatic waterfalls feature on this one-way tramp into Fiordland. For Milford Track bookings, contact Fiordland National Park Visitor Centre, P.O. Box 21, Te Anau.

Other popular tramping areas

The Waitakere Ranges and Hunua Ranges in Auckland offer fine tramping, with a full range of track lengths up to and including ones which require several days. All national and forest parks have well-defined tracks, from easy to difficult. Department of Conservation staff can advise on various day trips, according to fitness and experience.

Climbing

Climbing is never something to be attempted by the inexperienced in the absence of more experienced people. Information on climbing, rock climbing, ice climbing, mountaineering etc should be obtained from professional guides, local clubs or DOC. The main locations are in Tongariro National Park (Taupo), Egmont National Park (Taranaki) and the Southern Alps throughout the South Island.

Main DOC offices

Whangarei
P.O. Box 842. Tel: 0-9-438 0299
Auckland
Private Bag 68908, Newton.
Tel: 0-9-307 9279
Hamilton
Private Bag 3072. Tel: 0-7-838 3363
Rotorua
P.O. Box 1146. Tel: 0-7-347 9179
Gisborne
P.O. Box 668. Tel: 0-6-867 8531
Napier
P.O. Box 644. Tel: 0-6-835 0415
Turangi
Private Bag. Tel: 0-7-386 8607
Wanganui
Private Bag 3016. Tel: 0-6-345 2402
Wellington
P.O. Box 5086. Tel: 0-4-472 5821
Nelson
Private Bag 5. Tel: 0-3-546 9335
Christchurch
Private Bag. Tel: 0-3-379 9758
Hokitika
Private Bag 701. Tel: 0-3-755 8301
Dunedin
P.O. Box 5244. Tel: 0-3-477 0677
Invercargill
P.O. Box 743. Tel: 0-3-214 4589
Head Office
P.O. Box 10240, Wellington.
Tel: 0-4-471 0726

Several good books on the walkway system and longer tramps are available at booksellers throughout New Zealand.

Trees & Plants

KAURI

MATAI

RIMU

SILVER
FERN

KOWHAI

Trees & Plants

RATA

CABBAGE TREE

KAHIKATEA

POHUTUKAWA

Eye to Eye – Helen Casey

Trees & Plants

MIRO

MOUNTAIN
BEECH

TOTARA

MANUKA

NIKAU

Eye to Eye – Helen Case

26

Trees & Plants

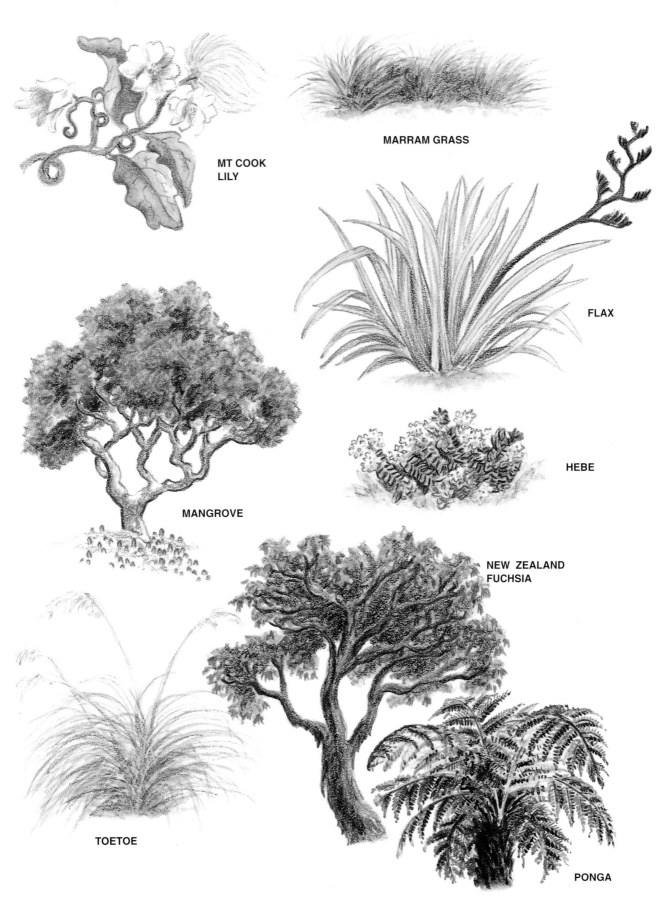

MT COOK
LILY

MARRAM GRASS

FLAX

MANGROVE

HEBE

NEW ZEALAND
FUCHSIA

TOETOE

PONGA

Bird Identification

BELLBIRD

TUI

KINGFISHER

NORTH ISLAND FANTAIL

SILVEREYE

SOUTH ISLAND ROBIN

NEW ZEALAND PIGEON

BROWN KIWI

Bird Identification

HARRIER HAWK

MOREPORK

KAKA

KEA

RED-CROWNED PARAKEET

PUKEKO

REEF HERON

WHITE-FACED HERON

Bird Identification

CASPIAN TERN

MUTE SWAN

YELLOW-EYED PENGUIN

SPOTTED SHAG

GANNET

WHITE-FRONTED TERN

BLACK-BACKED GULL

RED-BILLED GULL

30

Bird Identification

NEW ZEALAND DOTTEREL

BANDED DOTTEREL

PIED STILT

VARIABLE OYSTERCATCHER

GODWIT

DABCHICK

GREY DUCK

BLUE DUCK

31

Sheep Breeds

Wools of New Zealand

NEW ZEALAND ROMNEY

Wools of New Zealand

CORRIEDALE

Wools of New Zealand

SOUTH LEICESTER

Wools of New Zealand

PERENDALE

Wools of New Zealand

SOUTH SUFFOLK

Wools of New Zealand

NEW ZEALAND HALFBREED

Wools of New Zealand

MERINO

Wools of New Zealand

DRYSDALE

Cattle Breeds

JERSEY COW

AYRSHIRE COW

FRIESIAN COW

ANGUS HEIFER

HEREFORD BULL

Key-Light Image Library Ltd – G. Meadows

Key-Light Image Library Ltd – G. Meadows

Key-Light Image Library Ltd – G. Meadows

Key-Light Image Library Ltd – G. Meadows

AgResearch

Commercial Fishing Species

HOKI

BLUE COD

KAHAWAI

TREVALLY

GROPER

SAND FLOUNDER

TARAKIHI

SNAPPER

JOHN DORY

ORANGE ROUGHY

Commercial Fishing Species

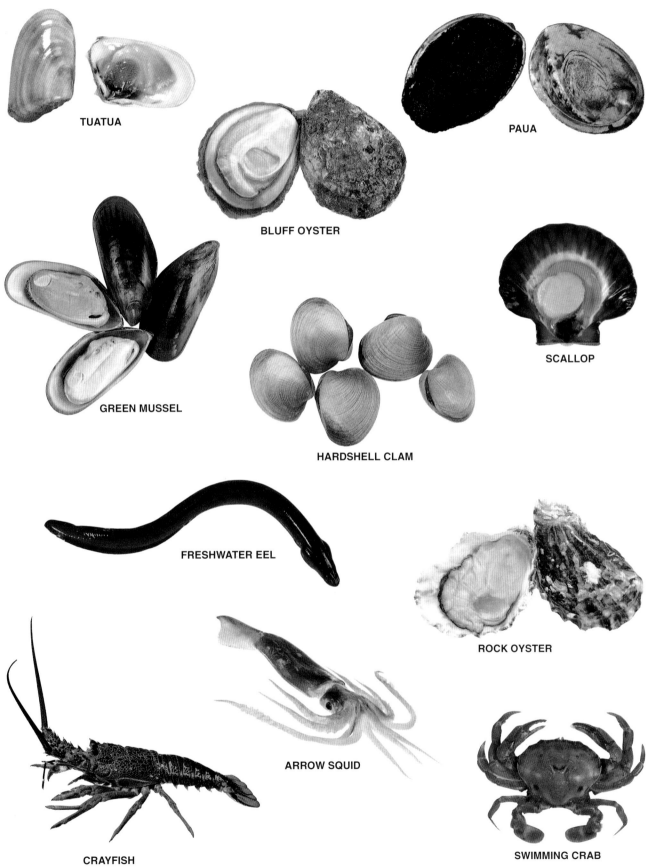

TUATUA

BLUFF OYSTER

PAUA

GREEN MUSSEL

HARDSHELL CLAM

SCALLOP

FRESHWATER EEL

ROCK OYSTER

CRAYFISH

ARROW SQUID

SWIMMING CRAB

NZ Fishing Industry Board

Whangarei

New Zealand's northernmost city sits between forested hills and a deep harbour which enables international oil tankers to dock at Marsden Point. The surrounding area is fertile farmland, with orchards and native and exotic forests, and the volcanic soil supports many beautiful parks and gardens.

Parahaki is New Zealand's largest Maori pa complex, with signposted walks and views of the city and harbour. Other features of the city include the A.H. Reed Memorial Kauri Park, Mair Park, the Margie Maddren fernery, and the Whangarei and Wairua Falls.

There are a number of art and craft centres as well as specialist museums, such as the quirky Clapham Clock Museum.

Nearby towns and attractions

Bay of Islands
The beautiful Bay of Islands, 70km north of Whangarei, was the first centre of European settlement in New Zealand, and is densely crusted with historical sites. It is a centre for big game fishing for marlin, tuna, and sharks, among the many islands which give the Bay its name. Maori chief Hone Heke lived and fought here, notably at Ruapekapeka, where military earthworks almost a century ahead of their time can still be seen.

Dargaville
The largest town on Northland's west coast, 58km southwest of Whangarei, Dargaville was founded on the kauri trade. Eighty percent of New Zealand's kumara (sweet potato) are grown on the river flats, and an annual Kumara Festival is held around harvest time.

The nearby coastline features unbroken golden sands for 100km, abounding with shellfish and ancient shipwrecks. Baylys Beach is popular for surfing, fishing and hiking, and the Kai Iwi Lakes to the north offer trout fishing, swimming and other waterborne activities. Active visitors can also climb the Toka Toka Volcanic Peak.

Here on the Kauri Coast one can absorb the whole history of the kauri, from seeing lignite reefs to visiting the Kauri Museum at Matakohe, with its displays of gum and timber milling. Then there is the glory of Tane Mahuta, the world's largest kauri tree, an hour's travel from Dargaville at Waipoua Kauri Forest. There are also night-time nature walks in Trounson Kauri Park.

Far North
Cape Reinga, 270km north of Whangarei, is, according to Maori belief, the departure point for the spirits of the recently deceased, who were said to climb down the twisted pohutukawa tree on the cliffs. There are views from the lighthouse, and walkways nearbay.

Doubtless Bay, 160km north of Whangarei, is a wide crescent of golden sand with a number of pleasant beaches. The historic fishing village of Mangonui is classified as a conservation zone.

Ninety Mile Beach, which starts 180km north of Whangarei, is a designated road, although it is not recommended for ordinary cars and the tides should be checked before starting out. There are bus tours available, some of which include a rollercoaster ride on the dunes at the southern end of the beach.

Kaikohe
Strategically sited on a plain 70km north of Whangarei, Kaikohe saw much of the warlike history of the north. The nearby Ngawha hot springs are said to have therapeutic properties. Shallow Lake Omapere is also fed by hot soda springs. Reed Memorial Park has a picnic site.

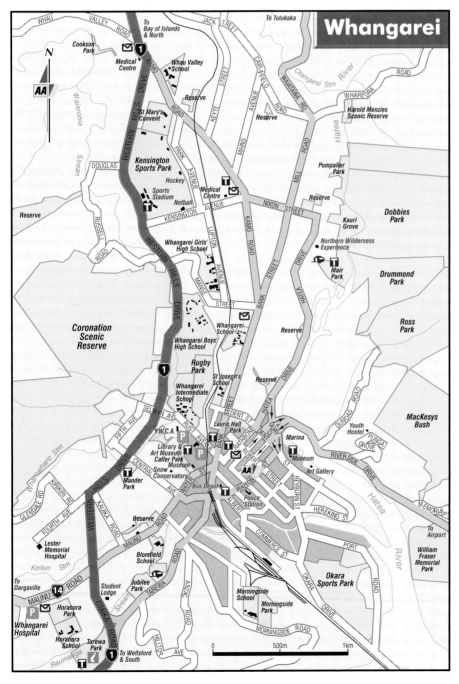

Whangarei

URUPUKAPUKA ISLAND, in the Bay of Islands.

Focus NZ – B. Moorhead

Kerikeri
A prosperous and photogenic region 75km north of Whangarei where citrus and tropical fruit are grown, Kerikeri is also well known for the local craftspeople and potters. The two oldest surviving buildings in New Zealand, the Kemp Mission House (built in 1822) and the Stone Store, are both in Kerikeri. Kororipo Pa and Rainbow Falls are nearby, and there is a reconstructed Maori village.

Marsden Point
New Zealand's crude oil refinery, processing oil from the Middle East and Taranaki, is located 30km southeast of Whangarei. In contrast to most such industrial operations, it is set in pleasant surroundings, the nearby beach being a popular swimming area.

The Refinery Visitors' Centre is open to the public daily, and features a working scale model and spectacular sound and light show (admission free).

Opua
The terminus for the car ferry which links Paihia with Russell, cutting out a long loop of winding road, is at Opua, 60km to the north of Whangarei. A steam train runs from Opua to Kawakawa through beautiful scenery.

Paihia
One of the earliest missionary centres, Paihia, 70km north of Whangarei, was the site of New Zealand's earliest church (no longer standing) and has a number of plaques erected along the foreshore by the Historic Places Trust. A ferry links Paihia with Russell, and a walkway leads to Waitangi. Cruises and game fishing boasts are based at the wharf.

Russell
This tranquil and beautiful little Victorian town, across the bay from Paihia, was once known as 'the hell hole of the Pacific' in the rough early days of European settlement, when its name was Kororareka. New Zealand's first capital was nearby. Christ Church, the oldest surviving church in New Zealand, is among the historic buildings. Flagstaff Hill provides panoramic views of the town and the Bay of Islands and a walkway leads to Ngaiotonga Scenic Reserve.

Tutukaka Coast
Fertile farmlands, beautiful beaches (especially glorious are Matapouri, Whale Bay and Sandy Bay) and spectacular sea views abound here, 26km east of Whangarei. The Coast is a base for diving trips to Poor Knights Islands Marine Reserve and for deep-sea fishing.

Waipu
Renowned for its Scottish heritage and traditions, Waipu, 40km south of Whangarei, was founded by Nova Scotian pioneers under the leadership of the Reverend Norman McLeod, and their arrival and settlement are commemorated in a local museum. Highland Games are an annual event on New Year's Day. Surfing and fishing are enjoyed in Waipu Cove, and the local caving club can provide access to Waipu Cave.

Waitangi
One of the most historic places in the country and connected by walkways to Paihia, Waitangi is one of the earliest sites of permanent European settlement in New Zealand, and the location of the signing of the controversial Treaty of Waitangi. Mt Bledisloe, nearby, offers unparalleled views of the Bay of Islands. Haruru Falls, connected by a bush walk to the Waitangi Treaty House, is a Maori canoe landing site and was New Zealand's first registered port. A museum and a superb golf course are among the other attractions.

Whangarei Heads
Spectacular castle-like peaks visible for kilometres, the Whangarei Heads are a beautiful part of Northland. The drive around such bays as Parua Bay leads to the white sands of Ocean Beach, to a climb of Mt Manaia, or an enjoyable coastal walk.

Auckland

A cosmopolitan city, Auckland holds nearly one-third of New Zealand's population in its sprawling suburbs. It is also one of the most spread-out cities in the world.

Auckland is known as the 'City of Sails'; the isthmus lies between two large harbours, the Manukau and the Waitemata, and the Waitemata gives on to the large, sheltered Hauraki Gulf. All sea-based water sports are enthusiastically pursued. Many of the islands of the Gulf are part of a large maritime park.

Ferry services to the islands operate from the wharf area in downtown Auckland, just across Queen Elizabeth II Square from the bottom of Queen Street.

Galleries, museums and other attractions

One of the best galleries in the country, with a collection of European Old Masters excelled only by the National Gallery of Victoria (Melbourne) in the South Pacific, the Auckland Art Gallery in Kitchener St has free admission except for special exhibitions. Frances Hodgkins, Colin McCahon and C.F. Goldie are New Zealand artists well represented here. There are also many private art galleries.

The Auckland War Memorial Museum, located in the Domain, with a commanding view of the city, has military and Maori history, natural history and geology.

Special interest museums include the Maritime Museum on Hobson Wharf, the Museum of Transport and Technology (MOTAT) at Western Springs. The International Rugby Hall of Fame is a new attraction, while Kelly Tarlton's Underwater World, Rainbow's End Adventure Park and the Expo Pavilion are also popular with people of all ages.

For wine lovers a trip to the vineyards northwest of the city is a must.

Historic buildings and sites

Alberton, at 100 Mt Albert Road, Mt Albert, is an imposing Victorian home, with towers and verandahs, furnished in period style and open to the public daily. Ewelme Cottage, at 14 Ayr Street, Parnell, is a spacious kauri cottage, designed and built by a well-known Auckland clergyman, Vicesimus Lush, in the 1860s. It contains much of its original furniture.

Highwic, at 40 Gillies Avenue, Epsom, is a colonial gentleman's mansion with fine, spacious grounds. Kinder House, at 2 Ayr Street, Parnell, is a gallery of the works of the nineteenth-century artist and photographer the Reverend John Kinder, including famous views of early Auckland. Much of Ponsonby, and in particular Renall Street, is also restored to its Victorian condition.

St Stephen's Chapel in Judge Street, Parnell; Selwyn Court, the beautiful wooden Cathedral Church of St Mary with its fine stained glass, and the controversial Holy Trinity Cathedral (Parnell); the chapel at St John's Theological College, St John's Road; and the stone churches of the central city are of interest.

Perhaps the most distinctive building in Auckland is the clock tower of the Old Arts Building. The attractive gardens of Old Government House on the corner of Princes Street and Waterloo Quadrant are near the newly refurbished High Court Buildings. A remnant of the fortified Albert Barracks Wall runs through part of the University grounds.

Parks, gardens and reserves

Auckland's isthmus is dotted with 48 extinct and dormant volcanoes, some of which are now quarried away, while others give their names to several suburbs. The

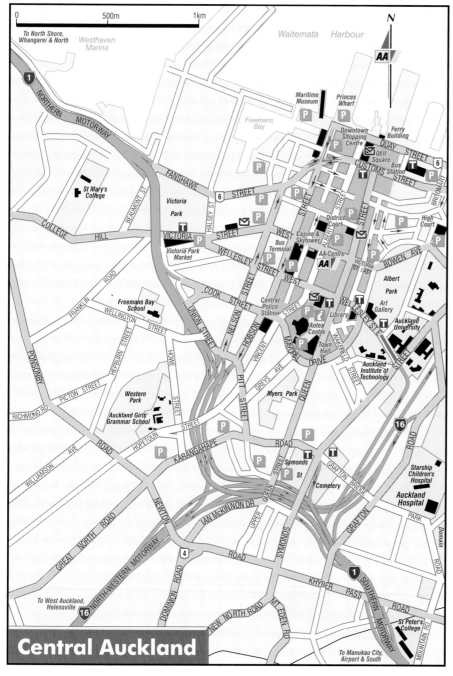

Central Auckland

Auckland

AUCKLAND INSTITUTE and War Memorial Museum.

of Queen Street and emerges on the Manukau Harbour at Beachcroft Avenue.

Auckland's many regional parks have a multitude of tracks and trails.

Shopping and markets

Besides Queen Street in downtown Auckland, Broadway in Newmarket is an important shopping boulevard while Parnell offers a shopping village in restored Victorian buildings. Covered and open-air stalls can be found at the Victoria Park Market and the Oriental Market, open daily. Both have a carnival atmosphere at weekends.

most famous, and those which give the best panoramic views, are Mt Eden and One Tree Hill.

Albert Park is a beautiful central-city park, with large old oak and Moreton Bay fig trees, a bandstand, statues, a large fountain, a floral clock and areas of bedding plants. Cornwall Park, farmland in the middle of the city, is planted with native and exotic trees and provided with picnic areas. It adjoins One Tree Hill Domain.

The Domain has been a popular reserve since Victorian times, with native and exotic trees, landscaped gardens, duck ponds, fountains, statuary and the beautiful Winter Gardens. Western Springs, to the west of the city, has landscaped ponds with water lilies and water birds. Adjacent to this is the Auckland Zoological Park. The Parnell Rose Gardens are considered the Southern Hemisphere's finest.

Reserves range from small, local playgrounds to the Hunua Ranges in the east and beautiful, accessible Waitakere Ranges in the west. There are a number of regional parks including farmland, bush, the Botanic Gardens in the southern region, and several coastal parks on both coasts.

Tamaki Drive

From the ferry terminal in Quay Street eastwards along the shore to Mission Bay, this is a pleasant walk or drive of 7km. The Savage Memorial Park on Bastion Point is not far beyond.

Walks and trails

Auckland is unique among world cities in having a coast-to-coast walk through its centre, which takes about four hours. It begins at the ferry terminal near the foot

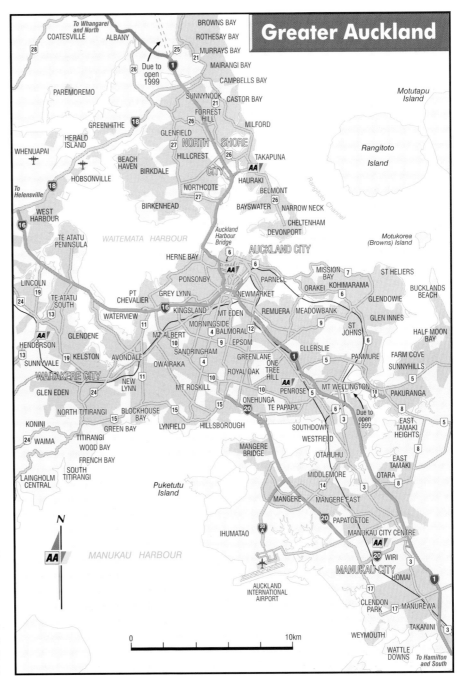

39

Auckland

AUCKLAND HARBOUR BRIDGE at sunrise.

Coromandel Peninsula

The Coromandel Peninsula, separating the Pacific Ocean from the Hauraki Gulf, is a beautiful, rugged area fringed with dozens of excellent beaches. Surfing, swimming, fishing and even in one case a hot stream under the sand are among the pleasures of these beaches, and in the water visitors can enjoy yachting, boating, kayaking and canoeing, water skiing, skin diving and snorkelling.

In the mountainous interior of the peninsula, forested and sparsely populated, tramping, rockhounding and horse trekking are popular pursuits. Behind Thames, the Kauaeranga Valley is a scenic and historic area, the scene of intensive logging last century. The forest park headquarters, 12km from Thames, displays a replica of the dams used to move kauri logs downstream and provides information on the many walks and picnic sites in the valley.

Many of the residents of the area are conservationists, alternative lifestylers and craftspeople, and there are flourishing craft trails in Thames, Coromandel and Whitianga, the larger towns. These, and a growing number of upmarket beach resorts, also offer activities such as tennis, golf, windsurfing, bowls, croquet, scenic flights and cruises, and hang-gliding.

The towns are of historical interest also, with fine Victorian buildings and relics of the goldmining and kauri logging days, both historic mining equipment (some of it operating) and local museums; there are Heritage Trails in all three towns. North of Coromandel township is the narrow-gauge Driving Creek Railway, set up by potter Barry Brickell.

Range roads

The Coromandel Range is crossed by four roads, linking the two coasts.

Coromandel to Whitianga direct (Route 309) is 33km of narrow, winding road through stands of native bush. Kauri Grove Scenic Reserve provides a short walk to a number of the magnificent trees. Nearby Castle Rock offers a spectacular view from the top, after a moderate climb, steep towards the top, taking about two hours for the return journey.

Coromandel to Whitianga via Kuaotunu (S.H. 25) is, at 50km, longer than the other Coromandel to Whitianga road. It is a winding road which climbs slowly, giving fine views of Coromandel Harbour, Whangapoua Harbour and Mercury Bay. The beach at the former goldmining town of Kuaotunu, on the way, is excellent for fishing, and there are glow-worms nearby.

Tapu-Coroglen Road is a rough, winding but highly scenic road of 29km, unsealed for most of the journey. A 'square' kauri tree can be seen 9km from Tapu.

Kopu-Hikuai Road (S.H. 25A), of 33km, is the newest and main crossing of the mountain range, deeply cut through rugged country and following an old horse trail of the gold-rush days at its highest point.

ROWBOATS at Whangamata.

Fotopacific – K. Wright

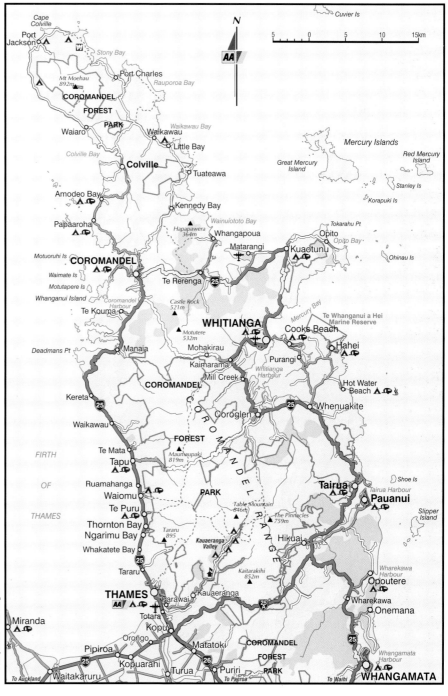

Tauranga

Tauranga, Maori for 'sheltered waters', is the largest residential and commercial area of the coastal Bay of Plenty. Fertile lands and warm climate make it the centre of a kiwifruit and citrus-growing area.

Numerous historic buildings and sites are preserved, such as the Gate Pa battle site, the Monmouth Redoubt, Otemataha Pa Military Cemetery, 'The Elms' mission house, and Tauranga Historic Village.

The parks and gardens of the area include Robbins Park, Strand gardens and Memorial Park. Kaiate Falls, McLaren Falls, Omanawa Falls, Minden Lookout, and several walkways are among the scenic attractions. There are also spec-tacular views from the Oropi-Oahuiti Road.

Papamoa Beach, to the southeast, is noted for its golden sand. Well supplied with amenities, Papamoa Beach is a relaxing retreat popular for surfing, surf fishing, beach walks and picnicking.

Maketu, a swimming and surf beach 45km southeast of Tauranga, via Te Puke, is a small holiday town. Te Ahioterangi and Whakaue meeting houses are nearby.

Waihi Beach, 19km north of Katikati, is a magnificent 10km surf beach. There are many walkways and pa sites in the vicinity and magnificent views from the road which runs up to the headland at Bowentown.

MT MAUNGANUI, to the south of Tauranga.

Focus NZ – B. Moorhead

Nearby towns and attractions

Katikati

The murals at Katikati, 40km northwest of Tauranga, reflect the town's historical background. The lookout at the top of Lindemann Road gives panoramic views from Bowentown Heads, a Maori pa site where the harbour meets the ocean. There is a swimming and surf beach here.

Katikati has a wealth of artists, potters, weavers and other craftspeople, and has won the Keep New Zealand Beautiful Best Small Town Award three years in a row.

Bush walks include a one-hour giant kauri tree bush walk, and fishing, mountain biking, horse riding, yachting, river walkways, and garden visits are among the other outdoor activities.

Mayor Island

This world-famous big game fishing centre is situated 35km off Tauranga, with marlin, tuna, kingfish and shark abounding in the surrounding water. The island was once a Maori fortified strongpoint. A marine reserve can now be found in the northwest corner of the island.

Mt Maunganui

'The Mount', 5km from Tauranga, is one of New Zealand's largest ports. It also has a very popular surfing and swimming beach. The fortification lines of a pa can still be seen on the Mount itself, from which there are panoramic views.

Te Puke

Te Puke, 31km south of Tauranga, is the 'kiwifruit capital of the world' as well as an area of attractive native bush. The Kiwifruit Country theme park offers guided tours around kiwifruit and horticultural plantings and jetboating may be enjoyed on the Kaituna River.

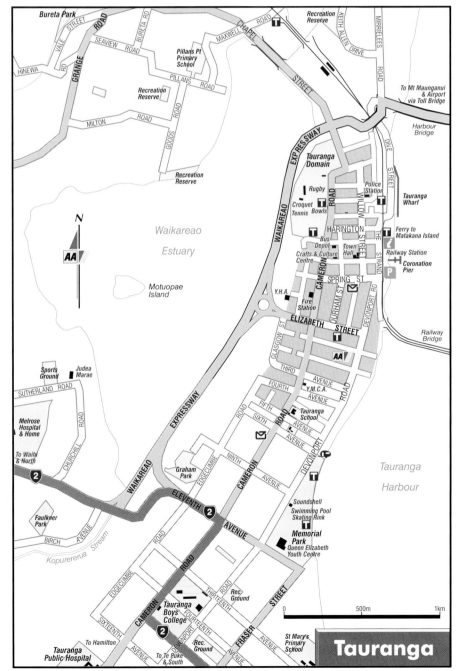

Gisborne

The sea coast and the Turanganui, Waimata and Taruheru rivers adjoin this prosperous, sunny river port city, giving it a pleasant aspect and leading to the name 'City of Bridges'.

Rich flat lands surround it, producing fine crops, while the hill country to south, west and north is prime beef, pork, lamb, mutton and wool production country. Maize is grown in vast quantities.

Galleries and museums

Several museums display relics of the past, and Wyllie Cottage is preserved as part of colonial history. For those with the skill to read it, Maori history and genealogy is recorded in the carved meeting houses Te Maua O Turanga (Manutuke), Te Poho Rukupo (Manutuke), Te Poho-o-Rawiri, and Rongopai (Waituhi).

GISBORNE.

Fotopacific – B. Moorhead

Historic buildings and sites

Nearby Matawhero was the site of the 'Poverty Bay massacre' by the renegade chief Te Kooti; only the Presbyterian church was spared from destruction. The Tairawhiti Heritage Trails take in this and many other historic sites.

Monuments associated with Captain James Cook include a Canadian totem pole (a gift for the Cook Bicentenary), the Kaiti Beach obelisk on Cook's landing site, Kaiti Hill (Titirangi Recreational Reserve) with its Cook statue, lookout and walkways, and the statue at Waikanae Beach of Nicholas Young (Young Nick), who was the first of Cook's crew to sight New Zealand.

Wineries

The first grapes in the world to see the morning sun are in the Gisborne area, which hosts a number of award-winning vineyards. The wineries are generally open for tasting during the summer but have restricted hours in winter.

Nearby attractions

Mahia Peninsula

A beautiful, barren, hilly promontory 65km south of Gisborne, with long, isolated golden sand beaches, the area is popular with campers, divers, swimmers, surfers, yachties, fishers and picnickers. There is a Department of Conservation information centre at Morere, nearby. Bush walks, fishing, garden visits, horse trekking, hot springs, skin diving, sailing and windsurfing are among the outdoor activities available in the area. There is an unusual rock baptismal font at Whangawehi.

Tolaga Bay

An attractive beach and location for picnics, set in sheep country 55km north of Gisborne. Captain Cook made two landings near here, in 1769 and 1777; on the first voyage, the official artist commented that the area was 'agreeable beyond description'. The wharf at the southeast end is famous as New Zealand's longest (660m). By previous permission from the manager of Hauiti Station, visitors can walk the 2km Cook's Cove walkway to see the 'Hole in the Wall' rock formation that so fascinated Cook's naturalist Joseph Banks. There is both sea and trout fishing.

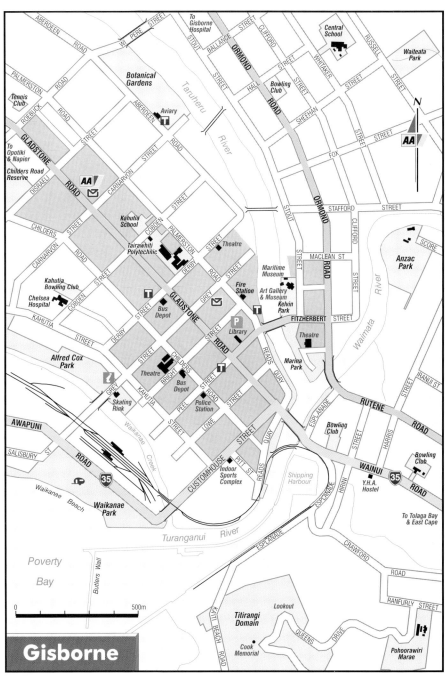

Gisborne

Napier & Hastings

The twin cities of Napier and Hastings were rebuilt almost from scratch in the 1930s after a disastrous earthquake. Napier in particular is proud of its many art deco buildings and newer developments often have art deco touches. The earthquake also raised the Napier harbour bed, and much of the inner harbour became rich farming land.

On the Heretaunga Plains 20km south of Napier, Hastings is the centre of a large fruit growing and processing industry, including winemaking. Hastings is the only city in New Zealand with streets laid out on the American block system.

The beach at Marine Parade, Napier,

ART DECO NAPIER.

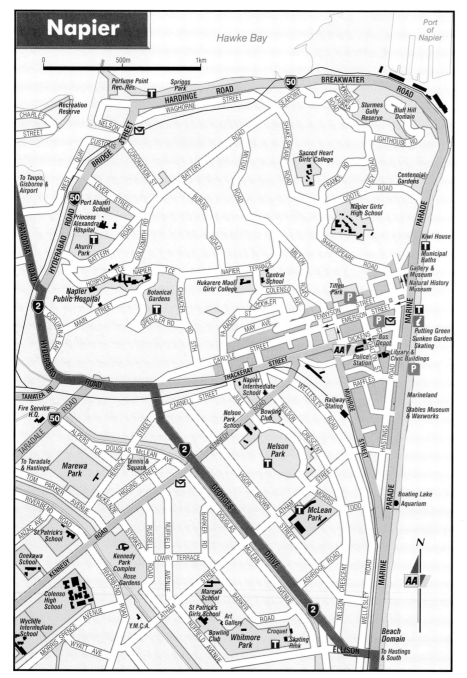

is not good for swimming, but several local seaside resorts offer surf swimming and sea fishing. Napier is the base for fishing trips and pleasure cruises.

Galleries and museums

The rich Maori and pioneer history of the area is well traced in the Hawke's Bay Museum at Napier, which has Polynesian and settler artefacts, earthquake history, paintings, books and photo collections, and one of the finest collections of Maori art in the world. St John's Cathedral Church has an interesting collection of memorabilia.

Historic buildings and sites

Both Napier and Hastings have dozens of art deco style buildings, and Napier's beautiful Marine Parade, lined with Norfolk pines, presents the maritime side of that city's heritage. Among the many attractions are the 'Pania of the Reef' and 'Spirit of Napier' statues, Lilliput village and railway station, the Kiwi House, Colonnade, Marineland, aquarium, gardens, fountains and sound shell.

Guided walks of the city are available in both Napier and Hastings.

Parks and gardens

In Napier the Botanical Gardens are near the centre of the city; other parks include McLean Park, Tiffen Park, Trelinnoe Park and scenic gardens, and the Kennedy Park rose gardens. Nearby Bluff Hill offers views of the area.

The pleasant parks of Hastings include Cornwall Park with its gardens, aviary and display house and Frimley Park, which has

Napier & Hastings

rose gardens, trees and a picnic area. The nearby rivers hold trout and are used for jet boating and white water rafting, while horse treks run into the surrounding countryside. There are long and short walks in the Kaweka Forest Park (50km northwest).

The Lake Tutira Bird Sanctuary is 40km north of Napier.

Wineries

Hawke's Bay is one of the main wine-making areas in New Zealand, where wines of growing international reputation are made. Many of the wineries have free tours or are open for visitors. Tastings are generally free, and wine may be purchased. About half the wineries also feature lunch restaurants, at least during summer.

The highlight for wine buffs is the annual Harvest Hawke's Bay festival, at Waitangi Weekend. During the weekend the Charity Wine Auction is held, involving the sale of locally made wine in barrels and oversized bottles, many of which have hand-printed labels, with all funds raised going to charity.

Cape Kidnappers

Thirty kilometres south of Napier is the world's most famous gannet colony, one of only two which can be approached from the land. As well as an 8km walk from Clifton to view the birds, journeys to the Cape may be made from Labour Weekend to Easter along the coast on tractor-drawn trailers or by four-wheel-drive vehicles overland.

Tide reports (free, but essential) should be obtained from the Visitor Centre if walking. At some states of the tide the journey is impossible; the official warning against falling rocks is also to be taken seriously.

In November and December up to 15,000 young and mature gannets may be seen here. The viewing season extends from late October to early April, the best times being early November to late February.

Nearby towns and attractions

Havelock North
Set in the foothills of the Havelock Ranges 5km southeast of Hastings and famed for its citizens' private gardens, Havelock North has a village atmosphere appro-

priate for the site of three of New Zealand's best-regarded private schools.

The largest honey processors in the Southern Hemisphere are located here, as are the oldest commercial wine cellars in New Zealand. Among the pleasant features of the town are the Keirunga Park Railway and several churches, including the contemporary Our Lady of Lourdes.

The finest views in Hawke's Bay can be obtained from the crest of Te Mata, behind Havelock North. The tranquil Tukituki river valley lies behind, while Havelock North and Hastings are laid out below. On a clear day, the view up the coast extends to

Napier and the Mahia Peninsula, and the Kaimanawa Ranges. The peak is also used for paragliding.

Norsewood
Norsewood, 85km to the southwest of Hastings, was settled by Scandinavian immigrants last century and retains some of its settler heritage, perhaps because the railway misses it and S.H. 2, while bisecting the town, also virtually bypasses it. Children occasionally perform traditional Scandinavian dances in the main street; the church and a Norwegian fishing boat are other remnants of Northern culture, also preserved in a museum.

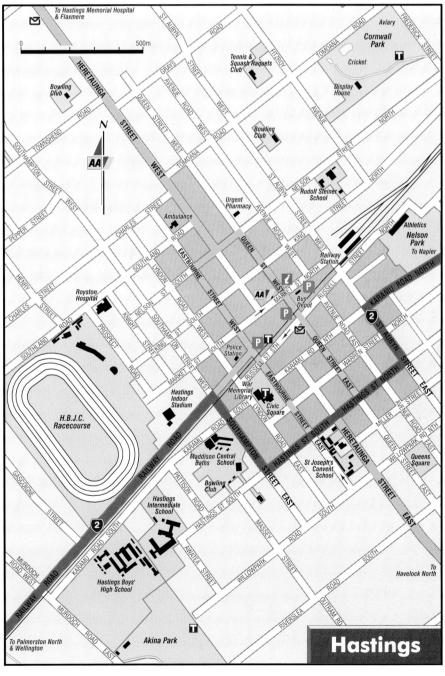

Hastings

Hamilton

There are cruises on the Waikato River, which flows through Hamilton, and much of the riverside is landscaped and provides enjoyable walkways. The city centre includes Ferrybank Park, the Founders' Memorial Theatre and fountain, the Hamilton Gardens (created in the Chinese style), Lake Rotoroa (used for yachting, boating and windsurfing), and Memorial Park with the steam tug Rangiriri.

The annual hot-air balloon festival has become a major drawcard, and each June the National Fieldays agricultural show, on a vast site at Mystery Creek, attracts farmers from all over the country.

The Waikato Museum of Art and History has an interesting building, houses important artefacts, and hosts exhibitions. The Waikato University campus is attractive. Agricultural research is carried out at nearby Ruakuhia and Ruakura.

Waikato River

The longest river in New Zealand flows from Lake Taupo over the Huka Falls, and gives its name (meaning 'flowing water') to the Waikato region. It reaches the sea at Port Waikato, not far south of Auckland. Once the major access route for the region, it is now the North Island's main source of hydroelectric power through a series of artificial lakes, also used for water sports. A number of the power stations offer guided tours.

Nearby towns and attractions

Cambridge
Cambridge, 24km southeast of Hamilton, is the centre of a rich farming and horse-breeding region, and polo is played locally. The town is well known for its antique and craft shops. Te Koutu Domain and Lake form a bird sanctuary, and panoramic views are obtained from Sanatorium Hill in Maungakawa Scenic Reserve.

Huntly
Huntly, 33km north of Hamilton, is known for its coal, used first by riverboats on the Waikato River and later by the power station. Other industries include brick-making (the distinctive orange 'Huntly brick' is famous).

Nearby, Rotowaro Bush Tramway runs old light steam trains on the first Sunday of each month (April to November). Pukemiro Junction has a large collection of industrial steam engines.

Natural features nearby include Huntly Lake (Lake Hakanoa) and the Whanga-marino Wetlands. The Te Tumu ancestral tree may be viewed (by permission) at Waahi Marae.

Karapiro
A hydroelectric power station operates on Waikato River water stored in this artificial lake, 35km southeast of Hamilton. The lake is a centre for water sports, and is used for major rowing competitions. There is a Domain and a lookout, and power-house tours are run.

Kawhia
A small, quiet, rural community, 80km southwest of Hamilton, Kawhia has an extensive Maori history; the Tainui canoe, used in the migration from the Pacific Islands, is traditionally believed to rest at Maketu Marae. The small but significant museum on the waterfront displays photographs, publications, artefacts and fossils of the region.

At Te Puia Ocean Beach (Hot Water Beach) hot springs well through the black sand, and between low and mid-tide visitors can scoop out their own hot pools. Fishing is enjoyed from the wharf and in the inner and outer harbours.

Marokopa Falls
Ninety kilometres south of Hamilton, the Marokopa River leaps over three falls, 6-12m high, and then a final, spectacular 36m fall. A ten-minute walking track from the road leads to the base of the falls. There are also many caves in the area.

Matamata
Situated on S.H. 27, 60km southeast of Hamilton, Matamata is the centre for many of New Zealand's thoroughbred horse studs and training stables, and one of the most productive dairy farming areas in the world. Some farms and studs may be visited by arrangement through the Information Centre.

Morrinsville
This is the dairy heartland of New Zealand, 30km northeast of Hamilton on the edge of the once swampy Hauraki Plains. Close by, Rukumoana Marae, site of the third Maori Parliament House, has been restored by the Historic Places Trust. Garden and craft tours run in the area. There are panoramic views from Mt Misery.

Ngaruawahia
At the confluence of the Waipa and Waikato Rivers, 19km northwest of Hamilton, Ngaruawahia serves as the Maori capital of the Waikato. The Maori Queen is based at Turangawaewae, 'the Place to Stand'. A regatta, featuring waka (Maori canoe) racing, is held annually on the nearest Saturday to 17 March, and the Turangawaewae Marae is open on this day.

SPECTACULAR night-time launch at Hamilton's Balloon Festival.

Focus NZ – B. Moorhead

Hamilton

Otorohanga

Set on fertile flats by the Waipa River, 60km south of Hamilton, Otorohanga is a farming and servicing centre for the district and a tourist base for Waitomo Caves. The famous Kiwi House has the largest outdoor atrium of native birds in the country, and a breeding colony of the rare tuatara lizard. Many of the local attractions are natural: garden trails, the Huiputea historic tree, kauri forest, and bush walks. The town is known for spinning, weaving and sheepskin products, and has the world's largest spinning wheel. Trout can be caught in the Waipa River.

Putaruru

Centre of the exotic timber trade in the Waikato, Putaruru, 65km southeast of Hamilton, is also known as New Zealand's Camellia Town and for its arts and crafts. Huge areas of forest stretch over the surrounding district.

Raglan

This peaceful town lies 47km west of Hamilton, by a fish-filled harbour. Black sand beaches are in summer crowded with swimmers and surfers enjoying the famous left-hand break at Whale Bay, Ocean Beach and Manu Bay. The Bridal Veil Falls and the Tattooed Rocks are among the features to be seen on walks in the area. Raglan Pioneer District Museum preserves the local history.

Te Awamutu

The main fame of Te Awamutu, 30km south of Hamilton, comes from its rose gardens, best seen November to April. Gardens include Memorial Park Gardens, and walks include the Pioneer Walk and tracks through Pirongia Forest Park. Selwyn Park is the site of the first mission station in the area, and St John's Church is noted for its stained glass. Other reminders of the past are the Te Awamutu and District Museum and the Waikato Railway Museum (open on the third Sunday afternoon of the month).

Te Kauwhata

Wine is still made locally in Te Kauwhata, 53km north of Hamilton, formerly a centre for government research into viticulture and winemaking. The Rangiriri battle site is nearby, and yachting and picnicking are enjoyed at Lake Waikare.

Te Kuiti

Known as the 'shearing capital of the world', Te Kuiti, 78km south of Hamilton, features a 6m statue of a shearer. It is the main town of the King Country, and a base for visitors to Waitomo Caves, 19km northwest. It also has a number of beautiful private gardens and public natural beauty in the Mangaokewa Scenic Reserve and the Pureora Forest Park with its native trees. There is a scenic walk along the riverbank, and the Wairere Falls and Totoro Gorge are nearby.

Tirau

Tirau, 55km southeast of Hamilton, is a small farming centre with an increasing number of antique shops. Garden walks may be taken and there is also a local honey industry.

Tokoroa

A huge pine forest surrounds Tokoroa, 86km southeast of Hamilton, and nearby is Kinleith pulp and paper mill. The hydro-electric lakes are used for boating, swimming and fishing, and there are bush walks in the forest and views from Colson Hill.

Waitomo Caves

A number of the Waitomo Caves, 75km southwest of Hamilton, are open to the public. Guided tours show visitors the magnificent limestone formations and the glowworm grotto of Waitomo Cave. Several caves are sites for adventure activities. A walkway runs nearby.

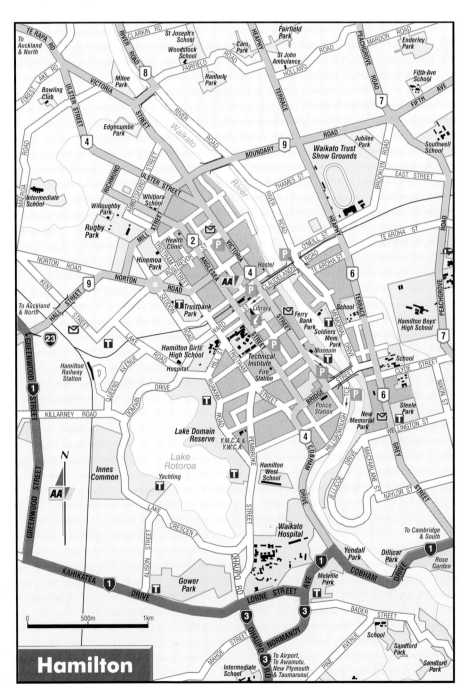

Rotorua

The 'city full of surprises' is the North Island's most famous destination for overseas visitors and an important cultural centre, known worldwide for its geysers, steaming lakes and streams, bubbling mud pools, multicoloured silica terraces and hot mineral pools.

Much thermal activity can be seen at Kuirau Park adjacent to the city centre. The park is a combination of a formal English garden and a thermal area with mud pools, hot springs and hot foot baths. Take extreme care – keep to paths at all times. Thermal features can also be seen at many places in the area, including Tikitere (Hell's Gate), Waimangu and Waiotapu.

The hospitable Te Arawa people are the Maori tribe mainly working in the tourist industry and a number of cultural demonstrations can be enjoyed by visitors, ranging from traditional carving and weaving to dances, songs and feasting from the traditional earth oven. Guided tours at Whakarewarewa include the Maori Arts and Crafts Institute, a Maori village and a thermal area with the famous geyser Pohutu.

Rotorua lies on the lake of the same name, one of a number of beautiful lakes in the area. Trout have been successfully released into the lakes, and at a number of parks the trout may be fed by hand.

Rivers flowing from the lakes are used for white water rafting and jet boating.

The event which literally shaped much of the Rotorua region occurred over a century ago, when Mt Tarawera erupted, destroying a nearby village and the famed Pink and White Terraces, and raising lake levels in a number of places. Four-wheel-drive, helicopter and light-plane trips to the now dormant Tarawera crater are possible.

Other attractions in Rotorua itself include the Bath House, Polynesian Pools, Orchid Gardens (complete with water organ) and the Maori cultural displays and hangis held at many hotels. Further out are the Skyline gondola and luge, the Agrodome and Trainworld.

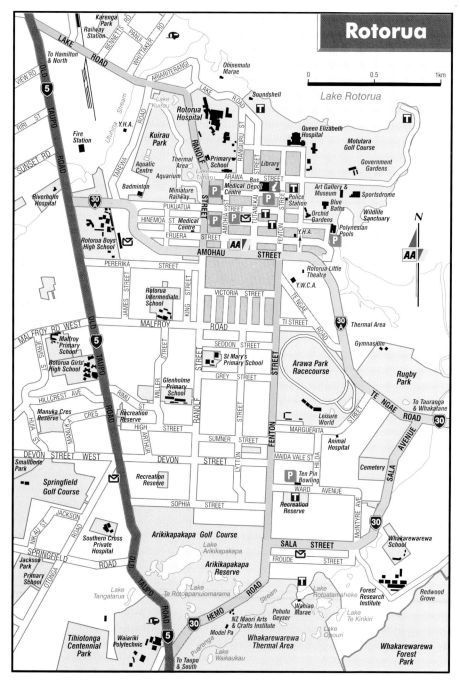

Historic buildings and sites

Ohinemutu, five minutes' walk from the town centre, was once the main Maori settlement on Lake Rotorua. St Faith's Anglican Church has a unique sand-blasted window, set so that Christ, dressed as a Maori chieftain, appears to be walking on the waters of the lake. The exterior is English Tudor and the interior decorated with Maori carvings and tukutuku woven panels. Gilbert Mair, a European officer admitted as an honorary chieftain of the Arawa tribe, is buried here.

Lookouts

Five minutes from the city centre, Mt Ngongotaha towers 778m above the city, with a lookout at the summit giving unmatched views of city, lakes and the surrounding landscape.

Adjacent to Lake Tarawera, Mt Tarawera exploded violently in 1886, killing 153 people, splitting itself open (there is now a 5km long crater), and burying Te Wairoa, the 'Buried Village'. It is now dormant. Te Wairoa Falls are among the natural features, and from the crater visitors can view more than 250km of scenery.

Walks and trails

Whakarewarewa Forest is a 3830ha multi-purpose forest, five minutes' drive from Rotorua city centre. The forest contains magnificent Californian redwoods, Douglas fir and other plantation trees. The Forestry Corporation Visitor Information Centre on Longmile Road contains displays, information and a woodcraft gallery. Forest walks can take from half an hour to all day, and there are also horse

Rotorua

CROQUET on the lawn at the Rotorua Bath House.

is small but considered the most beautiful lake in the area. There is a small holiday settlement, and the Blue and Green Lakes and Lake Tarawera are nearby.

Lake Okataina, 31km east of Rotorua, is one of the most beautiful lakes in the district, with its surroundings of native bush, including giant tree ferns. Glow-worms may be seen at night. Native fuchsia forms a canopy over the approach road, and in spring drops a carpet of red flowers. There are archeological sites, bush walks with native birds, a Lookout Rock, and sand and pumice beaches from which trout are caught.

The smaller of the two lakes from which Rotorua ('Two Lakes') takes its name, Lake Rotoiti, 12km northeast of Rotorua, is one of the most popular boating lakes in the area. A channel connects it to Lake Rotorua. It is bordered by bush and fringed with bays and beaches, picnic areas and the attractive Okere Falls, and swimming and trout fishing are enjoyed here. Nearby carved meeting houses may be visited by arrangement.

Fishing

Numerous professional fishing guides will take visitors to the premier trout fishing spots of Rotorua, where both fly fishing and trolling from charter launches yield excellent catches. Most will also smoke your catch for you, and some provide mounting of trophies. All equipment is available locally. Trout is not available commercially, and the only way to eat it is to catch it. A licence is necessary, and can be obtained from sporting goods shops or fishing guides.

and mountain-bike tracks, a nature trail and picnic areas.

Hongi's Track is reached 60km north-east of Rotorua between Lake Rotoiti and Lake Rotoehu. The northern warrior chief Hongi Hika returned from an audience with George IV in England with ideas of becoming a king himself. Part of this plan involved bringing men and canoes down this track to besiege the Te Arawa tribe on Mokoia Island in Lake Rotorua. The track is surrounded by magnificent bush, including the sacred tree of Hinehopu, and passes the Takaarewa Memorial Stone.

Lakes

The largest of the district's lakes, Lake Rotorua is nearly circular with Mokoia Island in its centre. A famous Maori love story had its setting on the lake; Hinemoa swam to the island to meet Tutanekai, her lover, guided by his playing of the flute. Tutanekai's flute, a Te Arawa taonga (treasure), formed from the arm bone of a tohunga (priest) and kept for years in the Auckland Museum, has recently been returned to the Te Arawa people. There are walking tracks on the island, where Hinemoa's Pool may be seen. Windsurfing and kayaking are among the activities enjoyed on the lake.

Eleven kilometres southeast of Rotorua are the Blue and Green Lakes. The markedly different Lakes Tikitapu and Rotokakahi lie beside each other, and are best seen from the lookout between them. The Green Lake, Rotokakahi, is regarded as tapu (sacred) because of the loss of a revered artefact in it. Many summer activities take place on Tikitapu.

Lake Okareka, 12km east of Rotorua,

THE CHAMPAGNE POOL at Waiotapu.

Taupo

This world-wide trout fishing mecca is situated at the outflow of the Waikato River from Lake Taupo. The approach from Wairakei offers spectacular views over the town, lake and distant mountains, and there is a pleasant lakeside walk, one of many in the area.

Anglers will find an abundance of fish in the lake and in the Waikato, Tongariro and Waitahanui Rivers and the many streams which flow into the lake. Trout were first introduced in 1884, and there is always good fishing somewhere. The colourful Karangahape Cliffs, visible across the lake, are best appreciated from a boat, in sunlight.

The quick-draining volcanic soil (pumice and ash) means that rain hardly ever spoils play on Taupo's six golf courses, all of which welcome visitors.

Thermal baths are open to the public, and many hotels have their own hot pools. Attractions such as Huka Village, which recreates Victorian times, and Cherry Island in the Waikato River are also popular.

Parks and gardens

Soldiers' graves from the wars of the 1860s are found 17km east of Taupo in the Opepe Reserve. A military redoubt, an old courthouse and a canoe are preserved at Taupo Domain.

A raised garden at Tongariro North Domain is filled with scented shrubs and herbs, for the enjoyment of the blind and partially sighted. Waipahihi Botanical Reserve contains alpine and native plants, with many rhododendrons and azaleas. There are views of the lake and mountains.

A native reserve, the 1099m Mt Tauhara, is administered by trustees appointed by the Maori Land Court. A walking track to the summit gives panoramic views of the central region.

Fishing

The Taupo fishing district, which includes the lake itself, offers unlimited potential to anglers at all levels of experience. Good trolling is possible on the lake year round, while many small streams entering the lake provide profitable evening fishing during 'smelting' between November and February. Anglers require a Taupo trout fishing licence, purchased for a day, week, month or season. These are available at numerous outlets in Taupo and Turangi including sporting goods stores, dairies, service stations, motels and hotels, and information centres.

Fishing is prohibited at all times from the Taupo wharf, boat jetties and the control bridge over the Waikato River.

Fly fishing only is permitted within a 300m radius of all stream and river mouths entering the lake, except the Waikino and Otupoto Streams and the Tokaanu tailrace. Nearly all rivers and streams in the district are restricted to fly fishing only. Fishing from a boat is prohibited within the same 300m radius of all rivers and streams entering the lake, except the Tongariro and Tauranga-Taupo Rivers and the Waikino and Otupoto Streams.

Trolling can be good all around the lake shore, from surface to deep down. Flies can be productive, but the best chance of success is with Toby lures and Tasmanian devils.

Equipment can be hired from several outlets, and fly fishing guides and charters can be arranged at the Information Centre. Guides (with all equipment and transport) range from $40-$45 per hour, lake fishing on a chartered boat with guide and all equipment from $60-$112.50 per hour for up to 10 people. Fishing licences additional.

Please check with local Department of Conservation officers, anglers, or sporting goods retailers to ensure that you are fishing within the law.

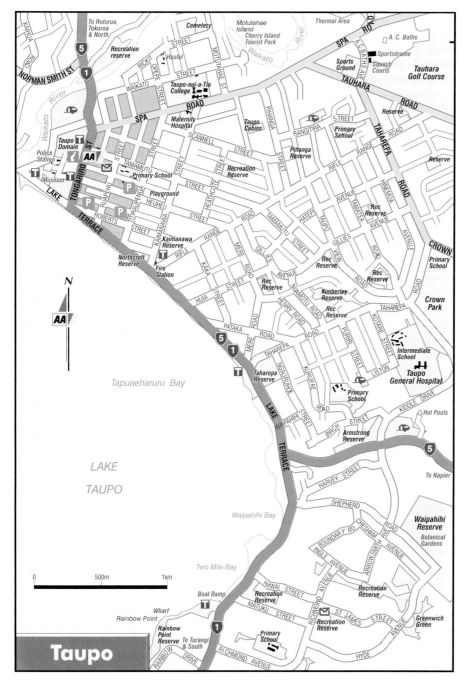

Wairakei

Large steel pipes cross S.H. 1 near its junction with S.H. 5, 9km north of Taupo, carrying underground steam for the geothermal power plant. This, the world's second large-scale geothermal power scheme, runs off groundwater seeping down to rocks heated by past volcanic activity. The Geothermal Visitor Centre provides displays and an audio-visual on the geothermal power schemes of Wairakei and Ohaaki.

At the Wairakei Prawn Farm guided tours take visitors around the geothermally heated fresh prawn farm, and north of Wairakei is the Orakei Korako thermal area.

Rapids and waterfalls

The flood-gates to the dam above the Aratiatia Rapids, 6km east of Wairakei, are opened daily at 10am and 2.30pm, and the rapids can then be viewed from the bridge or two lookouts.

Huka Falls, 5km north of Taupo, are probably New Zealand's best-known and most photographed falls. 'Huka' means 'foam', and not far from their source in Lake Taupo the blue waters of the Waikato River rush at almost 250,000 litres a second through a sudden chasm and leap over an 11m ledge, to foam mightily in a deep semicircular basin. The ledge is a result of ancient thermal activity. A bridge crosses the chasm just above the falls, and there are a number of viewing points on the other side.

Lake drive

Taupo is the largest town on Lake Taupo, but surrounding the lake's eastern shores are numerous delightful small settlements and scenic locales. In clockwise order, north to south:

Kinloch: a beautiful beach, bush walks, a marina, waterskiing, swimming.

Acacia Bay: lakeside walks, swimming, boating.

Waitahanui: excellent fishing, historically a major pa site.

Hatepe: a small river resort near Hinemaiaia Scenic Reserve (picnicking).

Motutere: scenic walks nearby, swimming, picnicking, fishing.

Te Rangiita/Oruatua: two attractive settlements divided by the Tauranga-Taupo River, popular for fishing and boating.

Motuoapa: a popular holiday spot with jetty, boat ramp and marina.

TROUT FISHING near Taupo.

Fotopacific – D. Hallett

Stump Bay: a perfect sandy curve, with lots of driftwood.

Turangi, at the southern end of the lake, serves the local forestry, farming and visitor industries. The visitor centre has an audiovisual display of the power scheme. Mt Pihanga, above the town, is such a beautiful mountain that the other nearby mountains were said in Maori legend to have fought over her, while the Tongariro River is one of the most famous trout fishing rivers in the world. The Department of Conservation runs a trout hatchery 5km to the south, with a viewing chamber and picnic and barbecue areas. Nearby Kaimanawa Forest Park offers hunting, tramping and picnicking, and Lake Rotopounamu (Greenstone Lake) is known for its bush, beach and birds. There is a viewpoint on the Pihanga Saddle Road. Turangi is also a base from which to visit Tongariro National Park and the ski fields within it.

Tokaanu: hot springs and fishing; the huge pipes above the town feed water to the hydroelectric power station; there are boiling mud pools, silica formations and geysers similar to those at Rotorua.

New Plymouth

The main city of Taranaki has diversified from a farming centre to a service city for various industries, including the local energy fields. The Taranaki gas and oil fields provide 40% of the Marsden Point refinery's feedstock. Until recently the port was the world's largest cheese export channel. There are several city walkways and Heritage Trails, as well as Te Henui Walkway. St Mary's Church is the oldest stone church in New Zealand.

Good local beaches are East End, Fitzroy, Oakura and Ngamotu. The city has three major festivals: the Festival of Lights, the Rhododendron Festival and the Taranaki Festival.

Egmont National Park is popular for skiing and tramping.

Galleries and museums

Those interested in New Zealand contemporary art should visit the Govett-Brewster Art Gallery, well known for its collection of Len Lye kinetic sculptures. The Taranaki Museum preserves historic artefacts.

Parks and gardens

There are many outstanding gardens open to the public in Taranaki. A festival in late October each year features 80-100 gardens open for inspection, of which many are open throughout the year. Rhododendrons and azaleas thrive in the volcanic soil of Taranaki, and the annual Rhododendron Festival involves more than 100 private and public gardens in late October each year. Pukeiti Rhododendron Trust is world famous for its beautiful grounds.

Pukekura Park, with its gardens, fernery, begonia house, and illuminated fountain and floodlit waterfall, is the finest in New Zealand and should be visited both by day and night.

Major viewpoints are Churchill Heights, Marsland Hill, Mt Moturoa and Paritutu Peak, while other parks include Brooklands Park with its outdoor sound shell, Kawaroa Park for picnics, Hempton rose garden, and Burgess Park (7km south). Lake Mangamahoe is known for its reflections of Mt Taranaki's peak.

Dawson Falls

A popular tourist attraction 902m up on the southeastern slopes of Mt Taranaki. The 18m falls were located in 1883 by Thomas Dawson, and are accessible by road.

Nearby towns

Egmont Village
At this small village centred around the turnoff to North Egmont, 14km southeast of New Plymouth, there are bush walks around nearby Lake Mangamahoe.

Eltham
A centre for the Taranaki dairy industry, Eltham, 53km southeast of New Plymouth, is famed for its many excellent cheeses. It offers access to the Dawson Falls, Egmont National Park, Kapuni gas field, Lake Rotokare walkway and wildlife refuge and Te Ngutu-o-te-manu battle site.

Hawera
A farming centre 74km southeast of New Plymouth by the inland route, Hawera is set on the Waimate Plain with Mt Taranaki dominating to the northwest. Nearby petrochemical fields provide another source of employment.

Te Ngutu-o-te-manu, 23km northwest, was the site of the battle in which Major von Tempsky was killed fighting Titoko-waru. It was in those turbulent times that New Zealand's only republic was declared in Hawera (and dissolved two weeks later when government troops arrived).

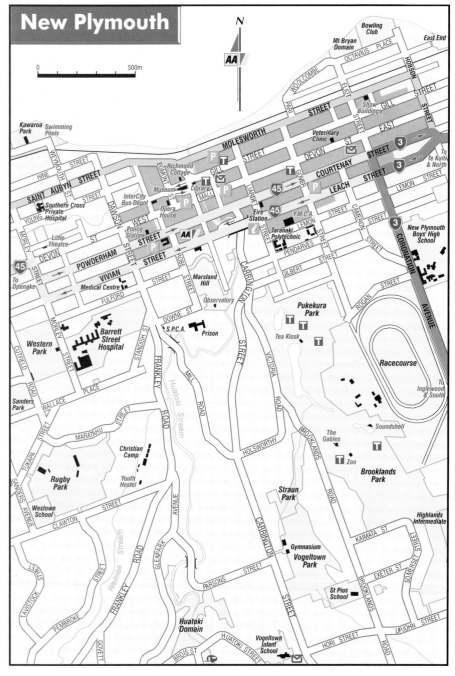

New Plymouth

The largest one-site multi-production dairy factory in the Southern Hemisphere is just outside the town. Also nearby are the historic pa Turuturu Mokai and Onawe Beach. The Tawhiti Bush Railway and Tawhiti Museum preserve the area's past.

Inglewood
Like other local towns, Inglewood, 22km southeast of New Plymouth, was originally a timber town but is now a centre of dairy farming. It is unusual in the number of different ethnic groups among its original inhabitants, including a large Polish contingent, Russians, Germans, Danes and others. Kerikeriringa Pa is 19km east and Pukerangiora Pa 8km northeast.

Okato
On the Stony River, 20km south of New Plymouth, Okato is known for trout and deep-sea fishing. The river is protected and good for swimming, and there is surfing and wind-surfing. Many tracks up and around Mt Taranaki begin here. Local artists and potters sell from their studios.

Opunake
A dairying centre, 62km south of New Plymouth, with farm tours available, Opunake is better known for the best beach in south Taranaki and for its sea fishing. Windsurfing is enjoyed at Kina Road Beach (10km north).

Stratford
A market town 43km southeast of New Plymouth and the access point for the eastern slopes of Mt Taranaki, Stratford was named for Shakespeare's birthplace. Besides King Edward Park, there are a number of private gardens open to visit. Stratford is a base for visits to the Dawson Falls, the Round the Mountain trek, and other activities in Egmont National Park. The Taranaki Pioneer Village preserves 50 historic buildings.

Waitara
The flat, fertile land surrounding Waitara, 16km northeast of New Plymouth, supports dairy farms, orchards, chicken factories, meat works and clothing manufacture. Several large energy projects include a methanol plant producing approximately 1200 tonnes per day, and the Methanex NZ Ltd gas-to-gasoline plant, which has an information centre. The many local activities include golf, horse riding, sea fishing, surfing and swimming. Outdoor activities are enjoyed around the Waitara River and beach. Among historic sites in the area are Manukorihi Pa and Owae Marae, and the Waitara Campaign Trail features battle sites of the New Zealand wars.

MT TARANAKI overlooks rolling farmland.

Fotopacific – E. Collis

Wanganui

Near the sea on the banks of the Whanganui River, 195km north of Wellington, Wanganui is one of New Zealand's oldest cities. Pleasant gardens brighten the city, especially in Queen's Park. Bason Botanical Reserve conservatory and gardens, Kowhai Park, Moutoa Gardens, and Virginia Lake's aviary, fountain, waterfowl, walks and winter gardens, Glenlogie Rose Gardens and the Bushy Park Scenic Reserve are among the other parks. There are views of the city and surrounds from the War Memorial Tower on Durie Hill.

The central business area provides areas for relaxing and entertainment. Castlecliff Beach features a Marine Parade, and deep-sea fishing charters, river trips, scenic flights and horse riding operate from the city. The Regional Museum has an excellent Maori collection, and the Sarjeant Art Gallery is strong on contemporary art and photography.

Historic homesteads and churches, including St Paul's Memorial Church (Putiki) with its Maori carvings, are found in the area.

Whanganui River

The second longest river in the North Island has its source in the snows of Mt Tongariro. The most beautiful part is upstream of Pipiriki, where 239 rapids make it popular for jet boating, while the outflow at Wanganui is suitable for rowing, windsurfing and yachting. Canoeists paddle downstream of Taumarunui in the summer. The historic Jerusalem Maori Mission is one of the famous sites on the river. The full-day drive along the river from Wanganui to Pipiriki and return is strongly recommended.

Whanganui National Park

The park straddles the Whanganui, although the river itself is not part of it. The rugged forest offers tramping and horse trekking to locations such as the Bridge to Nowhere, a disused bridge leading to abandoned farms.

Nearby towns

Patea
A market town, Patea is 60km northwest of Wanganui. The Patea River is navigable by launch. There is a riverside walkway, and another near Lake Rotorangi, where cruises and trout fishing are also enjoyed. The South Taranaki Museum holds items of local history. There is also a surf beach.

Waverley
Surrounded by fertile farmland, and near the rock stacks and caves of Waverley Beach, Waverley is 45km northwest of Wanganui. The Kohi Maori rock drawings are on private property nearby; directions and permission from the Library and Information Centre. Rewi Alley's cottage is preserved as a memorial to the pioneer of New Zealand-Chinese friendship.

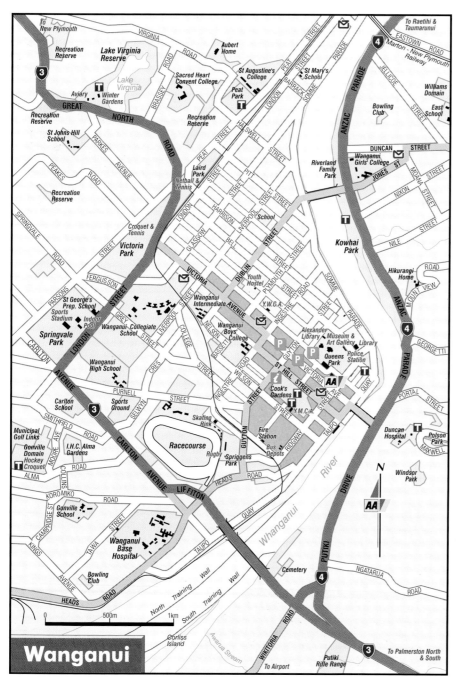

Fotopacific – J. Thorne

CANOEING on a tributary of the Whanganui.

Palmerston North

A pleasant provincial city, home to Massey University and the crossroads of the Manawatu, Palmerston North is set on the right bank of the Manawatu River.

The Square has the Info Centre, the Manawatu Community Arts Centre, the Manawatu Art Gallery, the Science Centre and Manawatu Museum, the Hopwood Clock Tower, a Cenotaph, gardens and fountains. History is found on Heritage Trails and at the Manawatu Country Life Farm Museum, Tokomaru Steam Engine Museum (19km south), and the White Pine Wildlife Park and Working Museum. The New Zealand Rugby Museum is a must for followers of the national sport.

THE SQUARE, Palmerston North.

On the river, sports include trout fishing, white water rafting and jet boating. Bledisloe Park has native bush, picnicking, and safe swimming, and Pohangina Domain (30km north) has native bush, walks, swimming and picnicking. Camping and tramping in the Ruahine and Tararua ranges can be enjoyed by the fit and horse treks are based in the city.

Linking Woodville and Ashhurst, the dramatic Manawatu Gorge road, which started out in 1867 as a bridle path, clings to the hill face and is in places supported by concrete piers jutting out of the rock wall. The road is a winding one, but short.

Nearby towns

Feilding
Feilding, 18km north of Palmerston North, is a properous rural centre. Beauty spots include Kowhai Park, Kimbolton Rhododendron Gardens (35km northwest), Kitchener Park bush (4km), Mt Lees Reserve (11km west), and the Mt Stewart Memorial viewpoint (8km southwest). There is trout fishing to the northwest.

Foxton
On the Manawatu River, 38km southwest of Palmerston North, this was once the Manawatu's chief port. It is now a service centre for farming communities. The Flax Museum, general museum and Trolley Bus Museum are worth a visit.

Levin
Backed by the Tararua Range, 57km southwest of Palmerston North, this is the centre of the Horowhenua region. Outdoor leisure is catered for at Kimberley Reserve, Lake Horowhenua (picnics, rowing and sailing), Tararua Forest Park and Waiopehu Scenic Reserve; there is whitebaiting at the river mouths.

Marton
A prosperous farming town and railway junction 40km northwest of Palmerston North, Marton has flower gardens, and St Stephen's Church is noted for its panelling. Dudding Lake Reserve (11km) has picnicking, swimming, boating and trout fishing. Vinegar Hill Reserve is near the town. To the northeast, Hunterville (28km) has a District Settlers' Museum.

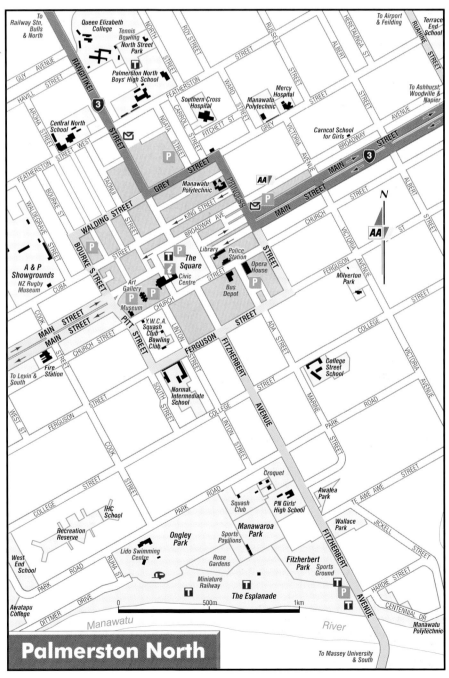

Focus NZ – D. Gray

Palmerston North

Wellington

Steep hills giving views of a spectacular harbour, the often rough waters of Cook Strait, and high winds interrupted by brilliantl, calm days form the setting for New Zealand's cosmopolitan capital city.

The geographical and political centre of New Zealand, Wellington boasts many museums, libraries, galleries and theatres. It houses Parliament and much of New Zealand's civil service and overseas diplomatic corps, as well as company head offices. It is home for the New Zealand Symphony Orchestra as well as the Royal New Zealand Ballet. The best of Wellington Harbour can be seen on a harbour drive.

Galleries, museums and libraries

The Museum of New Zealand (Te Papa Tongarewa) houses in one building, in Buckle Street, a museum and art gallery. The museum is strong in the fields of geology, palaeontology, botany, ethnology and colonial history. The carved Maori meeting house is said to be the finest example of its kind. The gallery displays New Zealand, Australian, British and European works of the 19th and 20th centuries. The New Zealand Academy of Fine Arts shares the facility. The new Museum of New Zealand is now being built on the waterfront and is to open in 1998.

The City Art Gallery is located in the old library, Civic Square, and features contemporary art, talks and cinema. The Dowse Art Museum, in Lower Hutt, holds exhibitions of New Zealand art.

The Maritime Museum in the Harbour Board Building, Queens Wharf, Customhouse Quay, displays a large-scale model of the harbour surrounded by paintings, prints, plans, photographs, cases of instruments, registers and memorabilia. The National Cricket Museum is in the Old Stand at the Basin Reserve.

Included in the National Archives, 10 Mulgrave Street, is the original of the Treaty of Waitangi. An exhibition gallery, reference service and historic photographs, and a Sound and Music Centre complement the National Library, at the corner of Molesworth and Aitken Streets, in which copies of all books published in New Zealand are lodged. The Alexander Turnbull Library is in the same building.

A major part of the world-class civic centre, at 65 Victoria Street, the Wellington Central Library is flanked by a colonnade of nikau palms sculptured in metal. The interior furnishings are also magnificent.

Historic buildings and sites

Antrim House, at 63 Boulcott Street, is a kauri mansion built in 1904. Ascot Street is a delightful hillside street preserving 'Old Wellington'. Colonial Cottage, at 68 Nairn Street, is a restoration of an 1858 cottage.

Katherine Mansfield is one of New Zealand's most highly regarded writers. Her birthplace, at 25 Tinakori Road, has been restored and is open to the public.

Old St Paul's Church, in Mulgrave Street, is a beautiful church in the Colonial Gothic style. It has been preserved as a location for the performing arts, and contains many memorabilia from a century's service as a centre of worship.

The Beehive in Bowen Street houses the ministerial offices, Prime Minister's department and cabinet room. Parliament's debating chamber is in Bowen House, open for tours seven days a week. The old Parliament Building is the second-largest wooden building in the world.

Parks and gardens

Established in 1869, the 26ha Botanic Garden Education and Environment Centre, access from the top of the cable-

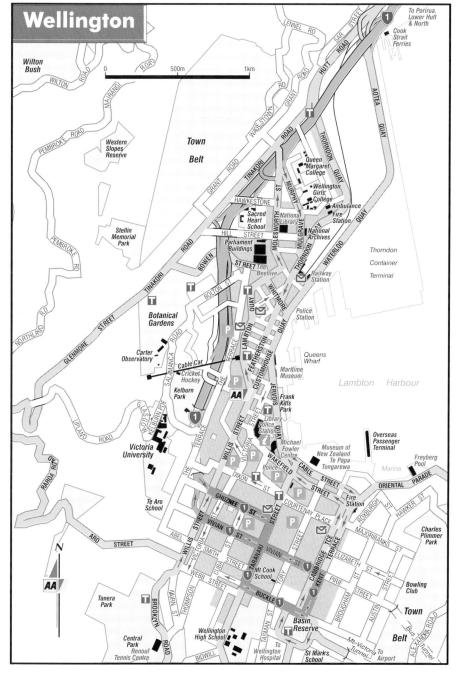

Wellington

A number of beautiful private gardens are open to visitors. Kapiti Island is a nature reserve, and day trips to it are available. Other activities include hang gliding, wind surfing, white water rafting, and bush and mountain walks.

The three notable museums in the area are the Paekakariki Railway Museum, where the atmosphere of The Engine Shed is designed to reflect that of a working locomotive department at the peak of the steam era, Southwards Car Museum, one of the largest private collections of motor vehicles in the Southern Hemisphere, and Wellington Tramway Museum in Paekakariki.

THE CABLE-CAR offers extensive views of Wellington.

car or off Glenmore Street, is the city's green heart.

Otari Museum of Native Plants, at 160 Wilton Road, is an ideal place to learn about New Zealand's flora.

Bolton Street Memorial Park is a central-city cemetery kept as a park. Frank Kitts Park in Jervois Quay is a downtown green spot on the waterfront.

Lookouts

The Lambton Quay cable-car to Kelburn (passing Victoria University) is one of only a few such rides in the world, and offers panoramic views of the harbour and the hills. The Hawkins Hill viewpoint has a wind turbine, part of an experimental electricity generation project. The best-known viewpoint, Mt Victoria, looks out on the city, harbour and Cook Strait and to the Hutt Valley. Perhaps the most exciting view is from the summit of Tinakori Hill, the site of radio transmission masts.

Hutt Valley

To the northeast of Wellington, the Hutt Valley's fertile plain is home to the major centres of Upper and Lower Hutt. Upper Hutt's attractions include the Silverstream Steam Railway, Tararua Forest Park and Staglands Wildlife Park (16km). Lower Hutt's attractions include the Dowse Art Museum, Jubilee Park and several Maori meeting houses. Also worth a visit is the nearby Petone Settlers' Museum.

Kapiti Coast

Beginning 30km north of Wellington Central, the Kapiti Coast stretches with pleasant beaches from the hills of Pae-kakariki to the undulating land of Otaki.

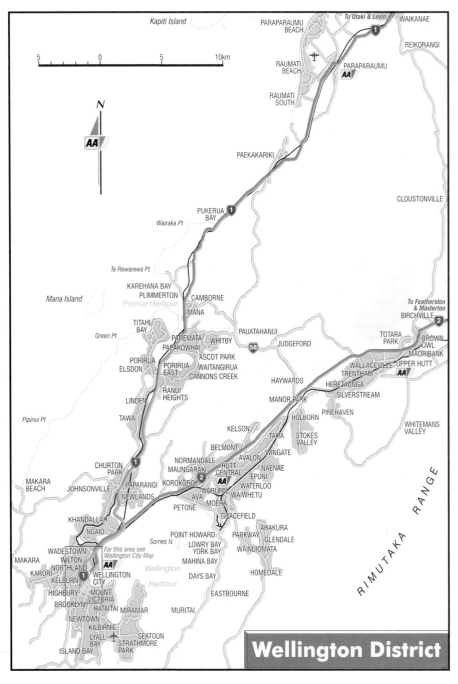

Wellington District

Blenheim

One of the sunniest towns in New Zealand, and famed for its wine, Marlborough's capital is situated on the Wairau Plains at the confluence of the Taylor and Opawa rivers.

The area produces wines that are among the best in the world. Tours to the wineries can be arranged; some have restaurants. There is an annual festival in February to showcase the industry.

The early appearance of the town is recreated at Brayshaw Museum Park. The Riverlands Cob Cottage has been restored as a museum. Tuamarina is the site of the Wairau Affray, a skirmish between Maori and settlers in 1843.

Seymour Square, near the modern town centre, has striking formal gardens, while a stream meanders through Pollard Park. There is an extensive craft trail. Other walks include the Wairau Lagoon Walk (7km south) and the Wither Hills Walkway.

Nearby towns and attractions

Havelock
On Pelorus Sound, Havelock, 41km northwest of Blenheim, is a tourist base and supply town. History is preserved in Carluke Pioneer Cottage (27km west) and the Havelock Museum. Gold-panning equipment may be hired at Canvastown (10km west). Fishing and sea kayaking are popular. The scenic road to Picton is well worth exploring, as are the Cullens Point Lookout and Walkway. Mt Richmond Forest Park extends to the southwest.

Kaikoura
This beautiful fishing town is 132km south of Blenheim. It is the New Zealand centre for whale watching, with daily tours available. Dolphins, seals, albatrosses and other wildlife can be seen.

Marlborough Sounds
The unspoilt islands and inlets of this drowned river system may be explored by boat, and there is camping at many reserves. Crail Bay Historic Reserve, Tennyson Inlet Scenic Reserve, Long Island and Kokomohua Marine Reserve, Maud Island and Stephens Island wildlife sanctuaries (a permit to land is required on these last) are all popular. The Queen Charlotte Walkway offers a number of walking/boating options.

Ship Cove, visited by Captain Cook, and Port Underwood are historic areas. The dolphin Pelorus Jack used to accompany ships through hazardous French Pass in the early years of this century, and his relatives play in the Sounds. The Outward Bound School is based at Anakiwa.

Picton
Deep in Queen Charlotte Sound, 28km from Blenheim, Picton is a port and tourist town. Part of the Marlborough craft trail, it is also a base for any number of water and land based tourist activities. Among the historic features of the area are the *Echo* historic wreck, the *Edwin Fox* clipper, and the Smith Memorial Museum. Nearby beauty spots include the Grove Road and Victoria Domain lookouts and the Karaka Point Reserve (8km northeast).

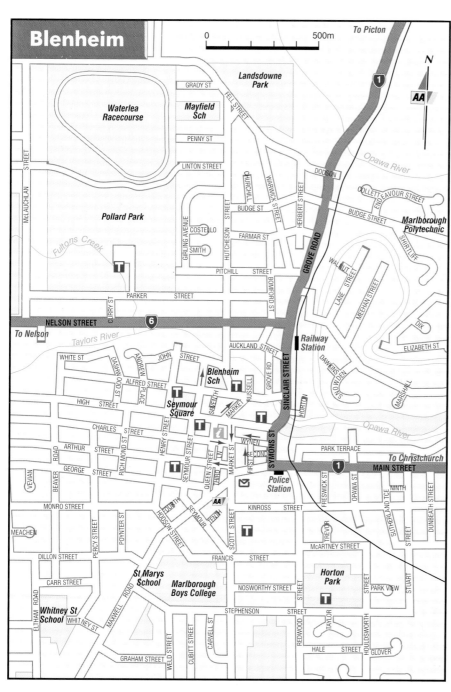

MARLBOROUGH VINES.

Nelson

This sunny, historic garden city is a centre for artists and craftspeople, especially potters. The early colonial architecture of the city is famous, as is the distinctive spire of the beautiful modern Christ Church Cathedral.

The range of activities available includes horse trekking, mountain biking, paragliding, rock climbing, and a wine trail. Walkers have the Cable Bay and Dun Mountain walkways, and the Maungatapu Track. The Northwest Nelson Forest Park and the Nelson Lakes Forest Park have many walking tracks, the best known being the Heaphy Track (see page 19).

Suter Art Gallery in Bridge Street has a small but fine collection. A 'Tourist Guide to Nelson Potters' featuring over 50 locations on a craft trail is available.

NELSON LEADLIGHTER in his studio.

There is a collection of Maori artefacts, documents relating to the early history of Nelson, and photographs at the Nelson Provincial Museum in Stoke. History is also featured in the Bishop's School and the Nelson Harbour Board Museum

Broadgreen House in Stoke, an early cob house (about 1855), has been furnished in period style. The chapel at Bishopdale, the Bishop of Nelson's residence, is open to the public.

The century-old trees shading rhododendrons and azaleas at Isel Park, Stoke, were brought by sea captains at the request of Thomas Marsden. The two-storey stone Isel House contains Marsden's family china and furniture.

Beauty spots include Queen's Gardens, Anzac Park, the Botanical Reserve, the Grampians and Flaxmore Reserve, the

Prince's Drive viewpoint (Davis Lookout), Rabbit Island beach, and the Scenic Drive. Tahunanui Beach is the main beach.

Nearby towns

Motueka

On Tasman Bay, 51km northwest of Nelson, Motueka is the country's most prolific orcharding region. Many artists and craftspeople work in the area. Motueka is a base for Abel Tasman and Kahurangi National Parks. Boating, jet boating, caving in the Ngarua Caves (21km west), craft trails, rafting, fishing, horse riding, horticultural tours, hunting, launch trips, mountain climbing, paragliding, sailing, scenic flights, sea kayaking, diving, swimming, tramping, water skiing and a wine trail are popular activities.

Kaiteriteri, 14km north, has stunning golden beaches and bays.

Marahau

Marahau, 20km north of Motueka, is a major tourist destination, and an entry point for Abel Tasman National Park. There is a Department of Conservation information centre. Horse trekking, kayaking, swimming with seals, a large beach, boating and tramping are among the activities.

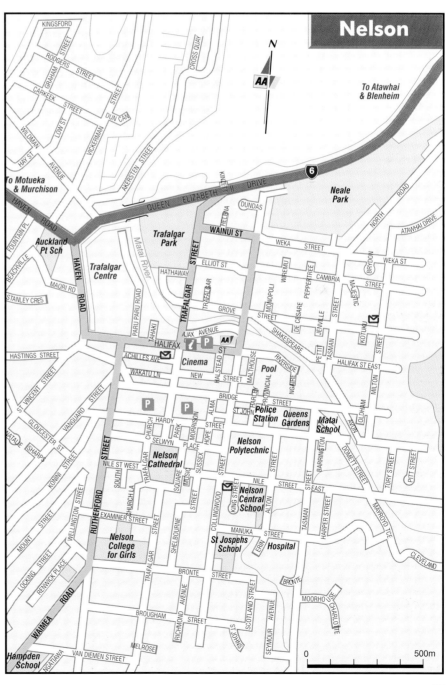

Focus NZ – G. Beal

West Coast

Rugged, green and wild, the West Coast in the 19th century drew people from all over the world to its goldfields. The original mining sites which scarred the landscape are now mainly overgrown, but some of the mining past is preserved in museums and recreations.

Outdoor activities include rafting, canoeing and fishing; there are also a number of limestone cave systems. The Buller area, in the north, considers itself the adventure centre for the Coast.

Tramping and mountain climbing are popular in South Westland. Much of the southern region of the Coast has been granted World Heritage status.

Towns and attractions

Charleston

An old goldmining town, 25km south of Westport, with the Mitchells Gully mine, just to the north, demonstrating the workings of a gold battery, Charleston is also a base for abseiling, fishing, caving, historical tours, rock climbing, underworld rafting and walking. Only 8km away, the Ananui limestone caves offer glow-worm displays.

Fox Glacier

This great tongue of ice, 202km southwest of Greymouth, is set in rainforest on the slopes of the Southern Alps. Most of the area's many walks can be done with average fitness and reasonable footwear. Walking on the glacier without a guide is not permitted. Other attractions are the Gillespie's Beach seal colony, a glow-worm forest, and Lake Matheson with its reflections of mountains. Scenic flights and helihikes are available.

Franz Josef Glacier

This spectacular, fast-flowing glacier, 180km southwest of Greymouth, is reached by a two-hour return walk. Visitors should not walk on the glacier without a guide. There are many walks, both short and long, in the area. Among nearby beauty spots are Lake Mapourika (9km north), which has trout and salmon, boating, swimming, birds and mountain reflections, Okarito Lagoon (20km north) where the white heron breeds, Peter's Pool (which is reflective) and Sentinel Rock. Notable buildings include the historic Defiance hut and St James' Anglican Church.

Greymouth

Greymouth was founded by goldminers and continues as a coal mining centre; it also has a significant timber trade. The port is the base for a large fishing fleet and is the principal centre for the West Coast. It is encircled by the 'Great Wall of Greymouth', a flood protection scheme.

The Brunner Industrial Site historic reserve, 11km east in the Grey Valley near Dobson, is the site of one of New Zealand's first major industrial complexes. The site can be reached over the old suspension bridge on foot or by car. Shantytown, 13km south, is the recreation of an old goldmining town.

Activities include bush walks, caving, gold panning, horse trekking, jet boating, river and sea fishing, scenic helicopter flights, scenic, white water and black water rafting, and tandem skydiving. In the town, there are brewery tours, a craft trail, the Great Wall walk and town clock, the Greymouth Art Gallery, the south breakwater offering mountain views, and the War Souvenir Museum of the RSA.

Haast

At the heart of the South West New Zealand World Heritage Area, 345km south of Greymouth, Haast is the location of the magnificent World Heritage Visitor Centre. A number of heritage sites have been constructed in the vicinity, and provide easy access to pristine rainforest, reflective lagoons, estuaries and long stretches of wilderness coast. Fishing, hunting, nature tours, scenic flights, scenic tours, tramping and unique flora and fauna are among the attractions.

Hokitika

Hokitika, 45km southwest of Greymouth, is world renowned for high-quality crafts. Greenstone, or New Zealand jade (pounamu), is found locally, and craftspeople work it into beautiful jewellery. The West Coast Historical Museum has goldmining equipment, scale models of aspects of gold recovery, a large collection of historic photographs and an audiovisual programme.

The high rainfall means that much of the local scenery involves water, and there is good freshwater fishing and whitebaiting. Beauty spots include the Hokitika River Gorge, Gibson Quay, the glow-worm dell, the Goldsborough walks and the Mahinapua Walkway (9km or 14km south). Kayak tours run on Lake Mahinapua and Totara Lagoon, and there are paddle boat cruises on Lake Mahinapua. Scenic flights run over the glaciers to the south.

THE WEST COAST's rugged and dramatic meeting with the sea.

Key-Light Image Library Ltd – B. Enting

West Coast

Karamea

The gateway to the Kahurangi National Park, set between the ranges and the Tasman Sea, 93km northeast of Westport, Karamea possesses a microclimate which enables subtropical fruits to be grown and permits tramping all year round.

Activities include walking, family rafting, the Cavern Creek cave system, helirafting, the Honeycomb Caves, kayaking, white water rafting, mountain biking, nature tours, scenic flights and fishing. Among nearby beauty spots are Lake Hanlon, the limestone arches of Oparara Valley, and Mt Stormy Track (by permission of Mt Stormy Farm). There is also a local museum.

Lake Brunner

In a glacier-scooped hollow 32km southeast of Greymouth, this swimming, boating and trout-fishing lake, Westland's largest, is surrounded by picnic spots. The township of Moana offers tourist services.

Lake Kaniere

Known for its beautiful light, this calm lake 18km from Hokitika often reflects forested hills and snow-capped mountains. Boating, water skiing, swimming and picnicking are all popular, with some fishing. The Hokitika River Gorge is well worth visiting for the beauty of the bush and the blue waters of the quiet river.

Paparoa National Park

The western slopes of the Paparoa Range above the small settlement of Punakaiki, 47km north of Greymouth, boast many gorges and limestone caves, a unique lowland karst environment, a wide range of geological features and lowland forest, and the famous Pancake Rocks and blowholes at Punakaiki. Activities include birdwatching, botany, camping, canoeing, caving, fishing, dolphin watching, surf boat tours, walking and swimming.

Reefton

Set in forested hills by the Inangahua River, 79km northeast of Greymouth, Reefton is very hot in summer and very cold and misty in winter. Victoria Forest Park holds many tracks which lead to old gold workings, and visitors may pan for gold in some areas. Reminders of the area's history are found in the Blacks Point Museum, a number of historic buildings, the School of Mines mineral collection and the Waiuta ghost town (38km). Activities include canoeing, gold panning, hunting, rafting, river swimming, walking and trout fishing.

Ross

Backed by the Totara and Makonui State Forests, Ross, 75km southwest of Greymouth, is further beautified by large rhododendrons and the blossoming cherry trees that line the main street. The 'Honourable Roddy', the West Coast's largest gold nugget (99 ounces), was found near here. The Jones Flat Walk takes in the site; the Water Race Walk passes the historic cemetery. Gold panning still results in small amounts of gold. The Ross Goldfields Visitor Centre includes an old mining cottage, displays, and a video. There is whitebaiting in the spring.

Westport

A sand beach, the steep Paparoa Range, the Buller River: this is Westport, 105km north of Greymouth. The architecture of the gold rush days has been well preserved. The imaginative Coaltown Museum is worth a look. There are a number of local walks. At Cape Foulwind, to the west, are a lighthouse and a seal colony. Activities include fishing, gold panning, horse trekking, jet boating, rafting, mine tours and mountain bike tours. Carter's Beach (good for surfing) and North Beach, Victoria Square gardens and the Westport Domain are other attractions.

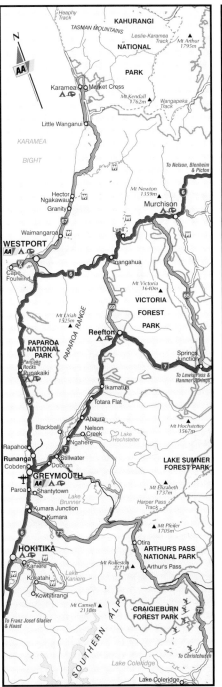
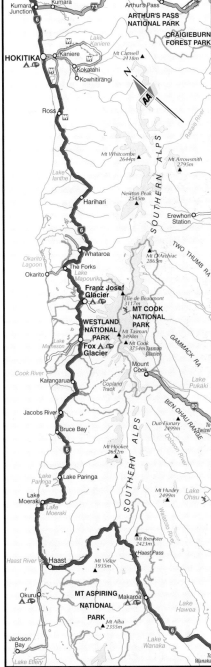

Christchurch

Known as New Zealand's Garden City, Christchurch was settled by English, mainly Anglican, settlers who arrived with the aim of creating an 'England of the South Seas'. Their use of stone in the English Gothic architecture of the cathedral and other buildings, the statues scattered about the city, the lazy loops of the Avon River, the English-style parks and gardens, and even the cold winters are all reminiscent of their homeland.

The grid pattern of the streets centres on Cathedral Square, where buskers, speakers and the eccentric Wizard of Christchurch may be heard and seen. Culture and entertainment are well provided for in Christchurch, which prides itself almost equally on its arts, its sports, its history, and its gardens.

Several different tours take visitors around the region by mountain bike, rail, coach, car or steamboat. There are also specialist tours of the city, hills and harbour, farm tours, garden tours, and wine tours to the small but excellent wineries in the Christchurch area. The Mt Cavendish Gondola whisks passengers from the Heathcote Valley to the top of the Port Hills for an all-round view.

Mt Hutt and other ski fields in the Southern Alps are within 1½ hours' drive of Christchurch.

Galleries and museums

Robert McDougall Art Gallery in Rolleston Ave features early and contemporary works.

Canterbury Museum in Rolleston Avenue features the Hall of Antarctic Discovery. Ferrymead Historic Park at 269 Bridle Path Road incorporates a recreation of a New Zealand Edwardian town. It has trams operating daily and steam engines at weekends and public holidays, a rural history museum and an exhibition of firefighting equipment.

Air Force World at Wigram accurately and creatively preserves the history of aviation in New Zealand, with 16 aircraft, many engines and items of equipment, plus hands-on exhibits, simulations, working models, theatrical presentations and Tiger Moth joyrides.

The International Antarctic Centre at the International Airport uses special technological effects to entertain and inform about Antarctic issues.

Other museums include Burnham Military Camp collections, Dr Hein's Classic Car Museum, the Lyttelton Historical Museum, the rugby, cricket and sports museum at Lancaster Park, the Science Alive hands-on science and technology centre, and the Yaldhurst Transport Museum.

Historic buildings and sites

The Historic Places Trust publishes a leaflet giving locations and commentary on 29 of the city's best buildings.

The Arts Centre, in the old university building in Worcester Street, caters for societies and individuals involved in performing, teaching or administering arts, as well as many art and craft activities, studios, shops and restaurants. A weekend market is held throughout the year.

The Canterbury Provincial Government Buildings in Armagh Street form the only provincial government complex still standing in New Zealand, government by provincial councils having been abolished in 1876. They are in Victorian Gothic style, built of wood and stone, with a wide variety of interior decoration.

Christchurch Cathedral, in the centre of the city, once dominated Cathedral Square. The view from the bell tower is still impressive, taking in a panorama of the city, the Port Hills, the plains and the distant Southern Alps. The Basilica in Barbadoes Street is considered New

Christchurch

Christchurch

SPRING at Christchurch's Hagley Park.

Zealand's most successful High Renaissance building.

The Town Hall in Kilmore Street is a widely admired modern building, with the much-photographed Ferrier Fountain on the south side. It provides fine concert and conference facilities for several thousand.

Parks, gardens and reserves

Well-known as a garden city, Christchurch boasts a number of beautiful parks, extensive Hagley Park being the best known. The Botanic Gardens with conservatories, rose and bulb beds, rock and water gardens, English lawns and woodland lie within Hagley Park, in a loop of the Avon River. A number of show houses display tropical, flowering plants, cacti and succulents, as well as ferns, alpine plants, bromeliads and orchids.

Other parks and gardens: Groynes picnic area, the Millbrook Reserve with its azaleas and rhododendrons, and Queen Elizabeth II Park (a major sports venue) all offer outdoor enjoyment. The garden at Mona Vale, on the banks of the Avon River, is open to the public, and Orana Park Wildlife Reserve has exotic and domestic animals roaming almost freely.

Nearby towns and attractions

Banks Peninsula
A volcanic peninsula, with two harbours (Lyttelton and Akaroa) in the eroded craters of the volcano, Banks Peninsula is a rural area next to urban Christchurch. The resort town of Akaroa was almost New Zealand's first French colony, and retains some of its French heritage in street names.

Beauty spots on the peninsula include the Ellangowan Scenic Reserve, Le Bons Bay (good for swimming), Little Akaloa (a small boat anchorage), Little River with its Birdlands nature reserve, Montgomery Park, Okains Bay (good for swimming, with a museum), Otepatotu Scenic Reserve, and Laveric Peak for views. To the south, Birdlings Flat is a beach known for the gemstones found there, and broad Lake Ellesmere, connected by a frequently reopened channel to the sea, is a haven for water birds, rich with eel and flounder.

Lyttelton
Christchurch's port lies 13km south of Christchurch beyond the Port Hills in an ancient crater on Banks Peninsula. The Bridle Path, over the hills, has been superseded by two tunnels (road and rail) through them, but it may still be walked. Lyttelton's Timeball Station, built in 1876, was used to signal one o'clock to ships. Launch and steam cruises on the harbour are available, passing Ripapa Island and Quail Island. On land are an Historical Museum, the Godley Head farm park and walkway, and Orton Bradley Park historic farm centre.

THE SIGN OF THE TAKAHE, with the Southern Alps beyond.

Timaru

A substantial city on gentle hills, above Caroline Bay, 164km southwest of Christchurch, Timaru has many stone and brick buildings. There is an art gallery, an aviary, botanic gardens and the South Canterbury Museum.

Farm tours, garden walks and industrial tours are available, and several local walkways as well as the Otaio Gorge scenic reserve (29km southwest) are popular. Notable buildings include an old wooden lighthouse, the Roman Catholic basilica, St Mary's Anglican Church and the Landing Service building. Sea fishing and yachting may be enjoyed in the harbour.

Nearby attractions

Fairlie
Fairlie, 62km northwest of Timaru, provides a base for skiing on Mt Dobson and the Two Thumb Range. Attractions include Burke Pass, Pioneer Park (20km southeast), walkways, fishing and museums.

Geraldine
A farming town 36km north of Timaru, Geraldine is close to historic sheep runs, Peel Forest Park and the Kakahu State Forest. The Downs road offers panoramas and there are prehistoric rock paintings at Hanging Rock, 29km away. Attractions

CUSTOMS HOUSE, Timaru.

Fotopacific – G. Baildon

include the Domain Gardens, the Rangitata and Opihi Rivers, Talbot Forest reserve, historic churches and museums.

Lake Pukaki
Mt Cook towers behind the glacial Lake Pukaki, 133km west of Timaru; the lookout view is particularly good. The lake is used for hydroelectricity and for fishing.

Lake Tekapo
Turquoise Lake Tekapo, 105km west of Timaru, has magnificent views. One window of the Church of the Good Shepherd frames the vista. Water sports, tramping and flightseeing are popular. Local bird sanctuaries and Mt John Observatory (6km) may be visited.

Mt Cook
Mt Cook National Park is a centre for mountaineering and ski touring. The famous Hermitage hotel, with spectacular views to Mt Cook, is located in Mt Cook Village, 70km north of Twizel.

Temuka
Temuka, 19km north of Timaru, is known for its ceramics industry. Fishing is another attraction. The Domain, Taumatakahu Stream walkway, the Courthouse Museum and the railway museum at Pleasant Point (15km west) are worth visiting.

Waimate
Waimate, 46km south of Timaru, is a centre for farming and horticulture. The white horse on the Hunter Hills honours the plough horses which broke in this land. Historical features include the Cuddy (an early building), St Augustine's Church, the Maori House shelter and rock drawings and Waimate Historical Museum.

Waitaki
The Waitaki Valley is 60km south of Timaru There are rock drawings at Duntroon. Lakes Aviemore and Benmore have boating and walking, while Lake Waitaki has boating. Goldmine tours are available. Ohau ski field has views over Lake Ohau.

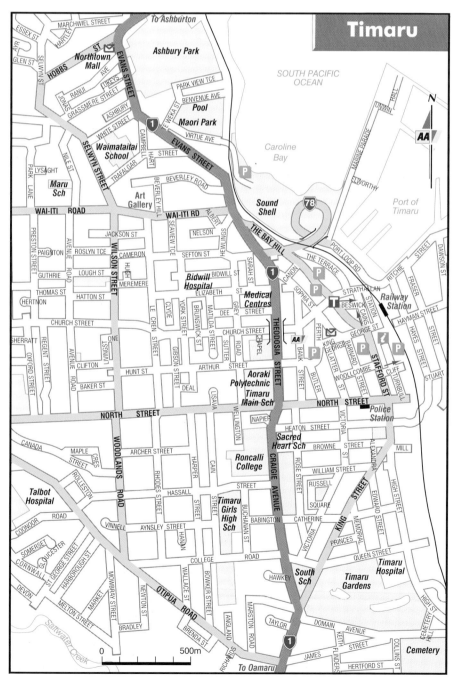

Dunedin

Bearing the Gaelic form of the name Edinburgh, Dunedin retains many Scottish influences. It still has a Victorian feel, with fine low-lying stone buildings rather than the towers of other New Zealand cities.

Dunedin is the capital of a sparsely settled region which once swarmed with gold prospectors. It is a city of culture and learning, distinguished by its university, the libraries, museums and galleries.

At the Otago Settlers' Museum, attractions include an 1860s cottage, a Cobb & Co coach and an intriguing selection of settlers' furniture. The Archives and Research Department is impressive and the museum's guided tours of the city are a rewarding introduction to historic Dunedin.

Of all New Zealand cities, Dunedin can boast the largest concentration of Victorian and Edwardian buildings. Dunedin's basalt and Oamaru stone railway station (1906) is one of the world's most photographed stations.The spacious foyer is decorated with Majolica tiles and a Royal Doulton mosaic floor. Stained-glass windows depict steaming locomotives, and the NZR cypher is found on almost every available surface.

UNIVERSITY OF OTAGO, Dunedin.

Focus NZ – J. Sprosen

Other buildings of interest are First Church, Olveston in Royal Terrace and the University clock tower in Leith Street. A detailed leaflet is available from the Information Centre in the Octagon, in the heart of the city.

The Botanic Garden covers 65ha and is situated at the northern end of the city. It is in two parts, the upper garden featuring native plants, an azalea garden, rhododendron dell, arboretum, aviary and visitor education centre, and the lower garden specimen trees, bedding plants, an alpine house, winter garden, conservatories, and a restaurant.

Lookouts include the Mt Cargill lookout, the Cargill Monument, the Northern Cemetery and Bracken's lookout, the Signal Hill centennial lookout, and the Unity Park lookout.

Nearby towns and attractions

Otago Peninsula
A green peninsula east of Dunedin with abundant wildlife, including the famous royal albatross colony and the rare yellow-eyed penguins. Broad views of city and countryside are crossed by old dry-stone walls on farmland. The Scottish Baronial-style Larnach Castle and a marine aquarium are among the attractions.

Port Chalmers
The historic port of Otago, 2km north of Dunedin has a precinct of 19th-century buildings, and structures of interest include the Anglican Church of the Holy Trinity, the St Mary Star of the Sea church, the Iona Church and the signalmast.

Oamaru
In the farming town of Oamaru, 116km north of Dunedin, the local limestone is used to fine effect in a number of buildings. The historic Totara Estate, the source in 1882 of the first shipment of frozen meat from New Zealand, is worth a visit. Coastal wildlife which may be seen nearby includes seals, yellow-eyed penguins, little blue penguins and Hector's dolphins.

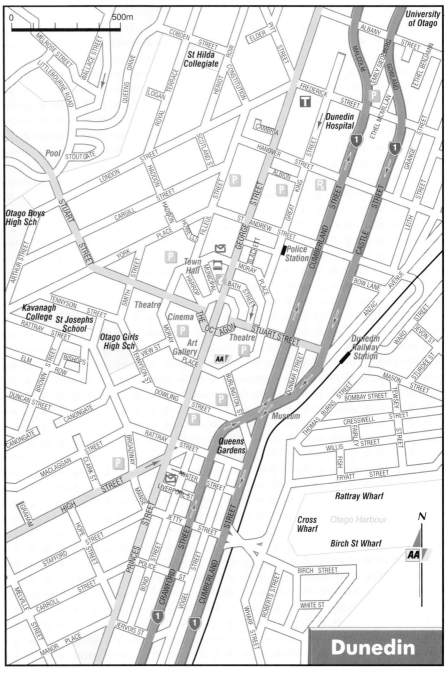

Queenstown

Originally a sheep run, Queenstown became a town in the goldrush days. The South Island's most popular resort, it is set on Lake Wakatipu among glacier-smoothed hills and rugged peaks. In winter it is a skiing centre and in summer visitors come to see the lake and take part in a wide range of outdoor activities.

Bobsledding, canoeing, curling, fishing, gold panning, hang gliding, hot-air ballooning, hovercraft, hydrofoils, ice skating, launch trips, mountain biking, paragliding, parapenting, rap jumping, river surfing, skiing, swimming, tame trout, tandem parachuting, trail rides, tramps, walkways, water skiing, white water kayaking and yachting are among the many adventure options.

There is an historical tour of Queenstown, which has an old stone library, a sound and light museum, an historic steamer wharf, and distinguished St Peter's Anglican church. The Skyline Gondola takes visitors to the top of Bobs Peak, which has a restaurant with a magnificent view.

Surrounded by firs and containing broad lawns and rose gardens, sporting greens and an open-air roller-skating rink, Queenstown Gardens are set on a glacial moraine peninsula. A large boulder bears the last words of Antarctic explorer Scott.

Some of the world's southernmost wineries are located near Queenstown. All are small, boutique wineries, and a tour is available.

Fiordland National Park (see page 16), with its magnificent sounds, is a few hours' drive away to the west.

Nearby towns and attractions

Alexandra

The largest town in Central Otago, Alexandra, 93km southeast of Queenstown, is the hub of New Zealand's stonefruit and merino fine wool industries. It is best known for the annual Blossom Festival and Golden Fleece shearing championships, both in September. An Olympic-size ice rink, gold panning, gliding, walkways, rabbit shooting and trout fishing are among the activities offered.

Features include a huge hillside clock, Manorburn Dam (30ha of natural ice skating), Old Man Rock (13km away), Shaky Bridge and the Tucker Hill lookout. History is preserved in the Sir William Bodkin Museum.

Arrowtown

Set beneath the rugged Crown Range, Arrowtown, 20km north of Queenstown, is a fascinating collection of mining cottages. The scenery surrounding the town is spectacular, and in April the exotic trees in the main street form a colourful background to a week-long festival recalling pioneer days. The Lakes District Centennial Museum and the Arrowtown Gaol display reminders of this era, along with the old cemetery and the Chinese quarter. Macetown is a ghost town 15km away, with access by foot, horse or four-wheel-drive. Gold panning still goes on in the area. Lake Hayes, Waterfall Park and the Memorial Hill viewpoint are among the many beauty spots.

Cardrona

A 25km drive from Wanaka leads through old goldmining areas, marked by sluicing activity, to historic Cardrona at the bottom of the Crown Range between Queenstown and Wanaka. The town is a base for horse treks and skiing, including Nordic skiing.

Coronet Peak

Some of the finest skiing in New Zealand is on the fine powder snow of Coronet Peak, 18km north of Queenstown. Heli-skiing is available. The Queenstown

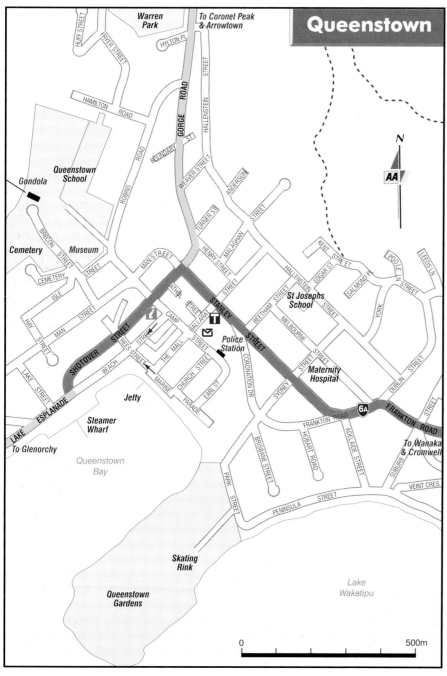

Queenstown

Winter Festival is held annually in early July. The stark surrounding mountains and valleys provide striking views year-round.

Cromwell

Historically known as 'The Junction' because of its location at the confluence of the Kawarau and Clutha rivers, Cromwell, 60km east of Queenstown, has developed into a service centre for an extensive farming and fruit-growing area. Redevelopment as an accommodation base for workers on the Clyde Dam project has meant that the town has a number of modern facilities and attractions, including buildings, indoor swimming pools, a polytechnic, golf, bowls and squash clubs.

The new Lake Dunstan behind the Clyde Dam has given the town boating, windsurfing, fishing, swimming and picnicking. Places to visit include the old mining towns of Bannockburn and Bendigo; Old Cromwell Town; Anderson Park gardens and arboretum. There is an annual Fruit Carnival (the last weekend in January).

The Information Centre has a museum, and the Old Cemetery and historic township also celebrate the district's past. Pottery and orchard tours run from the town. There are walks to Carricktown, Bannockburn Sluicings and the Old Reservoir, and the Cromwell Chafer Beetle Nature Reserve is beside the Bannock-burn-Cromwell Road. Greenways run through the town and give pedestrians and cyclists routes away from motorised traffic.

Crown Range

S.H. 89, between Queenstown and Wanaka, the highest main road in the country, starts 10km from Arrowtown and zig-zags up the Crown Range to 1120m. It offers many fine views along the way, including one of Mt Aspiring. The Cardrona Valley, much worked by miners, glitters with mica in sunny conditions. The road must be driven with care.

Glendhu Bay

A picturesque bay 12km northwest of Wanaka, with picnic spots and excellent fishing, it looks north across the lake to the Alps. The exotic trees provide summer shade and autumn colour. A road leads to the popular swimming area in the spectacular Motatapu Gorge, from which a track leads to Arrowtown.

Lake Wakatipu

Mountains rise abruptly from the shore of this glacier lake adjacent to Queenstown, with its unusual rise and fall in water level (about 12cm every five minutes in Bobs Cove). Wakatipu is New Zealand's third largest lake and boats of some size ply the deep waters; the most famous being the steamer *Earnslaw*, built in 1912.

Mt Aspiring National Park

Northwest of Wanaka and straddling the Great Divide is New Zealand's second largest national park. The rugged terrain includes active glaciers, hanging valleys, cirques and U-shaped valleys. Most of the alpine flora is unique to New Zealand, as are many of the birds. The Routeburn Track is one of many walks. Access from Wanaka is through the spectacular Matukituki Valley; Haast Pass to the West Coast also runs through the park. Besides tramping and climbing, boating, fishing and shooting are enjoyed in the park.

Remarkables

These towering mountains hold three basins developed into a commercial ski area. The peaks may also be climbed by a number of different routes; the most straightforward leads from the ski area, the most difficult directly up the Wakatipu face. A full day is necessary for the climb.

Skippers Canyon

The richest goldfield in the area, said to yield nearly an ounce of gold per square foot, was found here. Difficult access to this wild spot meant that very little profit was realised. Access is now by way of a high, narrow, winding road, which should only be attempted by very experienced drivers in good summer weather; coaches make the trip, when conditions allow, to Skippers Bridge, 100m long and 71m above the Shotover, a site for bungy jumping.

Wanaka

On the other side of the Crown Range, 70km northeast of Queenstown, Wanaka offers many adventurous diversions on the glacier lake of the same name. The view of the Alps across the gleaming waters, or reflected in them, is unparalleled. Wanaka is the gateway to Mt Aspiring National Park, the ski fields at Treble Cone and Cardrona, and the Waiorau Nordic Ski Area. The Clutha emerges as a full river from the lake's southern end, and Lake Hawea is separated from Lake Wanaka by a narrow neck of land, making Wanaka a centre for a wide range of water sports.

Focus NZ – P. Daly

T.S.S. EARNSLAW, the 'Lady of the Lake'.

Invercargill

New Zealand's southernmost city is set on open plains. The statue of the Blade of Grass acknowledges the source of the city's prosperity: pastureland.

There are art galleries, theatres, a museum, historic houses, a Maori carved meeting house, a 'tuatarium' (where tuataras are bred) crafts and pottery trail and an inner-city architectural walk.

Awarua Bay offers windsurfing, and the nearby wetlands offer birdwatching. At Curio Bay is a rare fossil forest. Fishing, horse riding, golf, the Scenic Drive, scenic flights and boat cruises are among the many activities. Beautiful Queens Park has an aviary, duckponds, rose gardens and a swimming pool with waterslides.

QUEENS PARK, Invercargill.

Nearby towns and attractions

Bluff

A port, fishing and service town, 27km south of Invercargill, Bluff is home to the Tiwai Point aluminium smelter (tours by arrangement). The fishing fleet includes dredgers for oysters, and the port serves as a link to Stewart Island.

Cruises, the Maritime Museum, the Paua House with its seashells, many seafood restaurants and a seafood festival (in mid-April) are among the attractions. The Foveaux Walkway runs nearby and there are views from Bluff Hill and Stirling Point Lookout.

Gore

Gore, 65km northeast of Invercargill, is surrounded by New Zealand's finest pastureland. A large brown trout statue and a Romney ram statue honour two of the major local features.

Gore hosts an annual country music contest and the South Island shearing championships. Attractions include a house made from old glass bottles, an air force museum, an art gallery, the Gore Historical Museum, a vintage car museum, a deer park, several golf courses, gardens and an aviary. There are walkways in

Dolamore Park. Trout fishing guides are available, and there is an ice skating rink.

Riverton

The oldest settlement in Otago-Southland, Riverton is a seaside resort and farming town 39km west of Invercargill. Activities include boating, duck shooting, fishing, jet boating and attractions include a museum, Observation Point, the Howell Memorial, a paua shell factory, and the Pourakino Walkway.

Stewart Island

With only one township, Oban, this island 32km south of Bluff has an unhurried pace.

Commercial fishing is the main economic activity, and salmon is farmed in Big Glory Bay. Much of the island consists of bush reserves, and tramping opportunities are limited to the northern part.

The world's southernmost golf course, brewery tours, diving, fishing trips, arts and crafts, guided nature trips, deer hunting, sea kayaking, kiwi spotting, mountain biking, parasailing, swimming with seals, tramping, underwater photography, walking and yachting are among the activities. There is an historic whaling base and a bird sanctuary. A maritime Mardi Gras is celebrated at Labour Weekend in October.

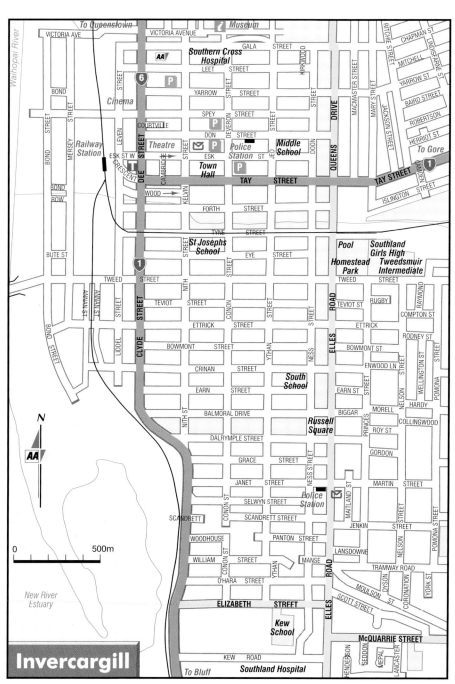

MAP SECTION

Stephen Robinson (Mt Taranaki)

Scale
1cm = 6km

Map
2

A   B   C   D

1

Kaiwi Lakes Walkway
Kaiwi Lakes
Lake Taharoa

Ahikiwi
Kairara
Maropiu
Avoca
Whatitiri
Wheki Valley
Otaika Valley
Otaika
Otuhi
Maungatapere Walkway
Puwera
Tamaterau
Parua Bay
Portland
One Tree Point
Mcleod Bay
Whangarei Heads
Taurikura
Ocean Beach
Urquharts Bay
Bream Head
Marotere Islands
Mamaranui
Maitahi
Waihue
Tangiteroria
Waiotama
Maungakaramea
Tangihua 627m
Pukehuia
Tangihua
TANGIHUA FOREST
Tangihua Walkway
Oakleigh
Takahiwai
Mata
Marsden Bay
Reotahi
Marsden Point
Bream Head
Omamari
Tangowahine
Hoanga
Omana
Pikiwahine
Mangapai
Moewhare
Tauraroa
Springfield
Ruakaka River
Ruakaka
Hen and Chicken Isl
Parore
Awakino Point
Windy Hill
Waiotira
Ruarangi
Waipu Caves
Taranga
Dargaville
Turiwiri
Waikiekie
North River
Braigh
Waipu
Waipu River
Bream Bay
Baylys Beach
Mangatara
Mt Wesley
Rehutai

2

Mahuta
Aratapu
Okahu
Taipuha
MARERETU FOREST
Mareretu
Waipu Cove
Langs Beach
Bream Tail
Mangawhai Cliffs Walkway
Te Kopuru
Tatararriki
Red Hill
Glinks Gully
Repia
Rehia
Parahi
Arapohue
Brynderwyn Hills Walkway
Cattlemount 430m
Mangawhai Heads
Tokatoka
Naumai
Whenuanui
Wairere
Brynderwyn
Tara
Mangawhai
Koremoa
Paparoa
Huarau
Maungaturoto
Pukekaroro
Tikinui
Raupo
Matakohe Kauri Museum
Matakohe
Pahi
Whakapirau
Marohemo
Kaiwaka
Hakaru
Te Arai Point
Ruawai
Mapau
Hukatere
Arapaoa
Tanoa
Te Arai
Spectacle Lake
Lake Tomarata
Taingaehe
Wairoa River
Manganui
Kaipara
Topuni
Tomarata

3

Rototuna
Kellys Bay
Tinopai
Port Albert
Oruawharo
Oneriri
Te Hana
Waiteitei
Whangaripo
Pakiri
North Head
Lake Humuhumu
Lake Rotokawau
Lake Kanono
Pouto
Kaipara Head
Wellsford
Hoteo North
Wharehine
Tapora
Wayby Valley
Wayby
DOME FOREST
Dome Forest Walkway
Whangateau
Big Omaha
Omaha
Omaha Flats
Matakana
Point
Takatu
Waiwhiu
Dome Valley
Sandspit
Kawau
Tauhoa
Streamlands
Kaipara Flats
Kourawhero
Woodcocks
Warkworth
Snells Bea
Algies Bay
Martins Bay
Mangakura
Atuanui 305m
Mt Auckland Walkway
Moir Hill Walkway
Moir Hill 358m
Hepburn Creek
Pohuehue
Mahurangi W
Glorit
Ahuroa
Pukapuka
Komokoriki
Puhoi
Araparera
Tahekeroa
Waiwera
Hot S
Whang
Mahurangi Harbour

4

Waioneke
Kakanui
Makarau River
Makarau
Puhoi
Due to open 2003
Waiwera
Hatfields Beach
Orewa AA
Makarau River
Shelly Beach
Kanohi
Wainui
Red Beach
Stanmore Bay
Lake Kereta
Kaukapakapa
Waitoki
Silverdale
Manly
Parkhurst
Hot Springs
Loch Norrie
Dairy Flat
Stillwater
Whangap
Okura Bush Wal
Okura
Long Bay
Parakai
Te Pua
Helensville
Redvale
WOODHILL FOREST
RIVERHEAD FOREST
Coatesville
Albany
EAST COAST BAYS
Wharepapa
Waikoukou Valley
Paremoremo
Ra
Woodhill
Riverhead
Huapai
Cuthill
TAKA
Rewiti
Greenhithe
Whenuapai
Hobsonville
Waimauku
Kumeu
AA

5

Taupaki
Waitemata
Muriwai Beach
Waitakere
Massey
Te Henga-Goldie Bush Walkway
Ranui
HENDERSON
Swanson
Te Henga (Bethells Beach)
WAITAKERE RANGES
Waiatarua
Titirangi
Mangere
Anawhata
Parau
Puketutu Is
Laingholm
Piha
Karekare
Huia
Cornwallis
Little Huia
Manukau Harbour
MANUKAU
Whatipu
Wattle Bay
Orua Bay
Big Bay
Grahams Beach
Manu
Weyn

6

Awhitu
Te Hi
Awhitu Central
Matakawau
Clarks Beach
K
Pollock
Waiau Beach
Waiau Pa
Patuma
Te Toro
Glenbrook Beach
Kohekohe
Glenbrook
Waipipi
Lake Pokorua
Tauranganaru
Pueko
Kariotahi
Waiuku
Whiriwhiri
Aka Aka

Map

2

1

E F G H

2

Mokohinau Islands

Port Abercrombie Channel

Motairehe
Kawa
Okiwi
Rakitu Is
Port Fitzroy
Kaikoura Is
▲ Mt Hobson 627m

▲ Mt Hauturu 722m
Little Barrier Island

Great Barrier Island

Whangaparapara
✈ Claris
Okupu

3

Craddock Channel

Colville Channel

Cuvier Is

Fletcher Bay
Port Jackson ●
🏕 Coromandel Track
Stony Bay
Port Charles
Port Charles
▲ Mt Moehau 892m
COROMANDEL FOREST PARK
29

4

ritiri Matangi Is

Hauraki Gulf

Waiaro
Waikawau
Little Bay
Colville Bay
Colville
Tuateawa

Mercury Islands
Great Mercury Is
Red Mercury Is
Kawhitu or Stanley Is

Amodeo Bay
28
Papaaroha
Kennedy Bay
Kennedy Bay
▲ Hapapawera 364m
Whangapoua
Whangapoua Harbour
Matarangi
Otama Beach
Opito Bay
Kuaotunu
Opito
Ohinau Is

Rakino Is
Motutapu Is
Motutapu Farm Walkway
Palm Beach
Oneroa
Onetangi
Waiheke Island
Stony Batter Walkway
Pakatoa Is
Motuoruhi Is
Coromandel
Waimate In
Motutapere Is
Te Rerenga
🛣 25
29
Mercury Bay

Blackpool
Surfdale
Ostend
Omiha
Rotoroa Is
Whanganui Is
Coromandel Harbour
▲ Castle Rock 521m
Whitianga
Cooks Beach
Hahei
Purangi

CKLAND
Orapiu
Ponui Island
Kauri Grove
▲ Motutere 532m
Kaimarama
Mill Creek
Hot Water Beach
Hot Springs

iOWICK
Beachlands
Maraetai
Tamaki Strait
32
COROMANDEL
Coroglen
Whenuakite
25

5

Whitford
Wairoa River
Pakihi Is
Kereta
Waikawau
Maumaupaki 879m
▲
🛣 25
The Aldermen Islands

atoetoe
Brookby
Kawakawa Bay
Orere Point
Orere
Te Mata
Waihou
Tapu River
Tapu
Ruamahanga
FOREST
Shoe Is
Tairua
Pauanui
Tairua Harbour

PAPAKURA
Red Hill
Alfriston
Ardmore
Clevedon
Aroaro Stm
Matingarahi
Firth
Waiomu
▲ Table Mountain 846m
Billy Goat Track
The Pinnacles 759m
▲
Hikuai
Slipper Is

Drury
Opaheke
Hunua
Ponga
Runciman
Cosseys Reservoir
Kohukohunui 688m
HUNUA
Upper Mangatawhiri Res
Wharekawa
Whakatiwai
Te Puru
Thornton Bay
Ngarimu Bay
Whakatete Bay
of
25
▲ Kaitarakihi 852m
PARK
TAIRUA FOREST
Wharekawa
Wharekawa Harbour
Opoutere

Ararimu
RANGES
Mangatangi Reservoir
Kaiaua
Thames
Taruru
Kauaeranga
21
25
Onemana

6

erata
Paparimu
▲ Mangatangi 487m
Viking Track
Happy Valley
Thames
Totara
Parawai
Waihou River
Kopu
Tairua River
Wharekawa

kekohe
East
Bombay
🅿🅿 Mt William Walkway
Mangatangi
Miranda
Hot Springs
Pipiroa
Orongo
Matatoki
26
Whangamata Harbour
Whangamata

ukekohe
Harrisville
hangarata
Pokeno
35
Maramarua
Kopuku
Maramarua Mill
Ratoroa 323m
Waitakaruru
24
25
Turua
Kopuarahi
Puriri
Omahu
COROMANDEL
Waiharakeke

Tuakau
Mercer
Maramarua
Ngatea
Wharepoa
G

⬇ 3

E F G H

Map 3

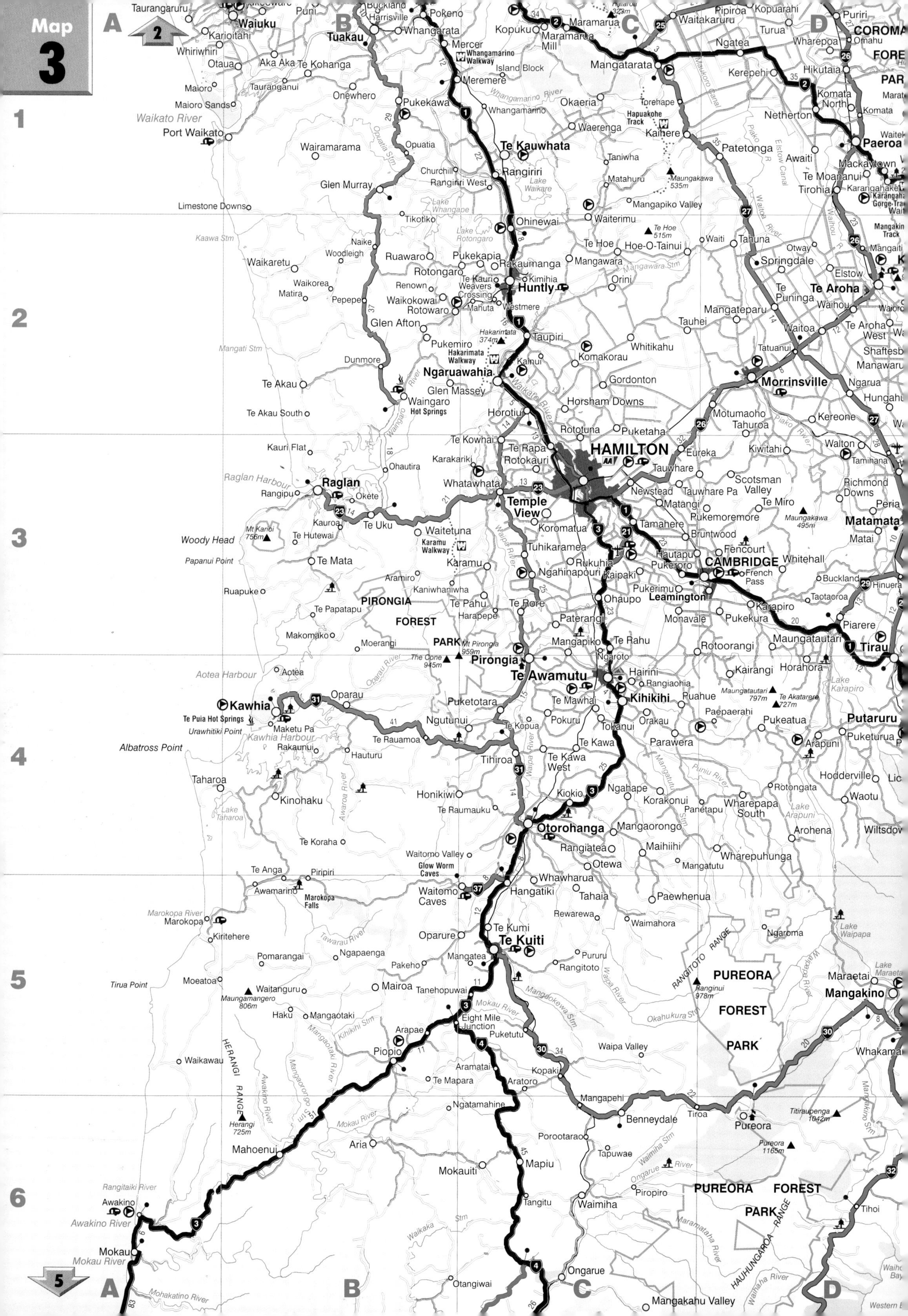

A | **B** | **C** | **D**

1 2 3 4 5 6

Taurangaruru, Waiuku, Karioitahi, Whiriwhiri, Otaua, Maioro, Maioro Sands, Waikato River, Port Waikato, Limestone Downs, Aka Aka, Te Kohanga, Tauranganui, Onewhero, Wairamarama, Opuatia, Pukekawa, Puni, Harrisville, Whangarata, Pokeno, Mercer, Meremere, Island Block, Whangamarino, Okaeria, Kopuku, Maramarua, Maramarua Mill, Waitakaruru, Pipiroa, Kopuarahi, Turua, Wharepoa, Puriri, Omahu, COROMA, FORE, PAR, Ngatea, Kerepehi, Hikutaia, Komata North, Komata, Netherton, Patetonga, Paeroa, Mackaytown, Waitete, Awaiti, Te Moananui, Tirohia, Karangahake

Waikaretu, Woodleigh, Naike, Ruawaro, Rotongaro, Pukekapia, Rakaumanga, Ohinewai, Waerenga, Waiterimu, Te Hoe, Hoe-O-Tainui, Waiti, Tahuna, Otway, Springdale, Elstow, Te Puninga, Mangaiti, Mangaiti Track

Huntly, Taupiri, Ngaruawahia, Glen Massey, Waingaro Hot Springs, Horotiu, Te Kowhai, HAMILTON, Morrinsville, Te Aroha

Raglan, Okete, Te Uku, Waitetuna, Karamu, Temple View, Cambridge, Leamington, Matamata

Kawhia, Te Puia Hot Springs, Pirongia, Te Awamutu, Kihikihi, Otorohanga, Putaruru

Te Kuiti, Waitomo Caves, Piopio, Pureora Forest Park, Mangakino, Mokau, Awakino

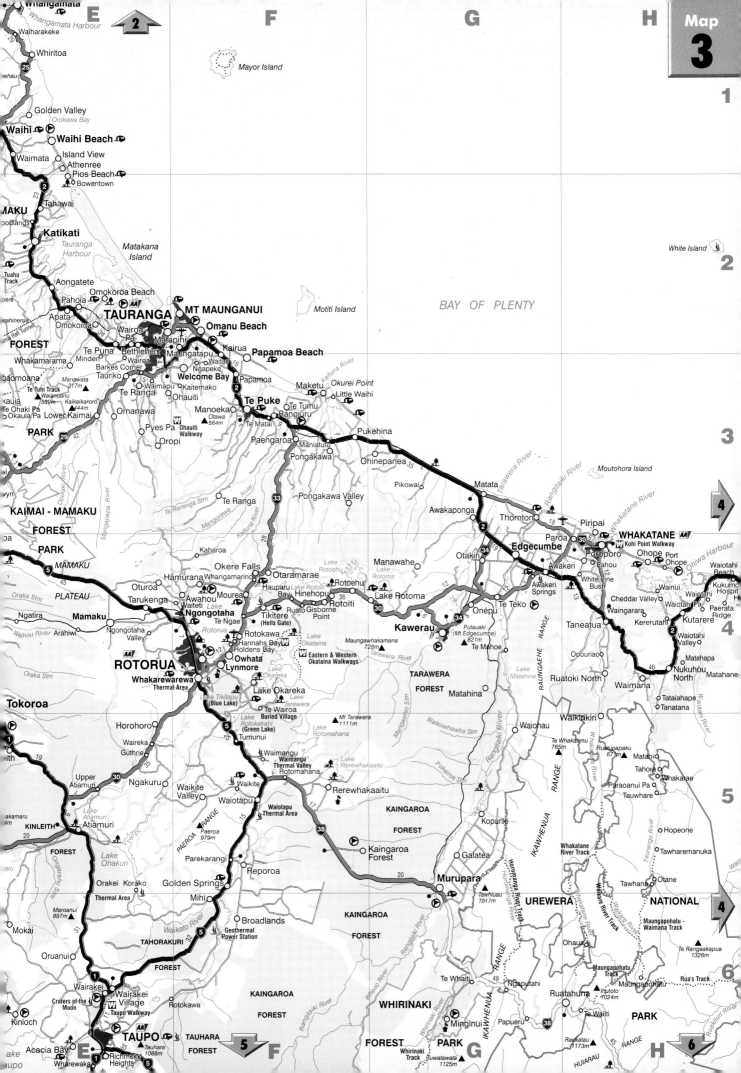

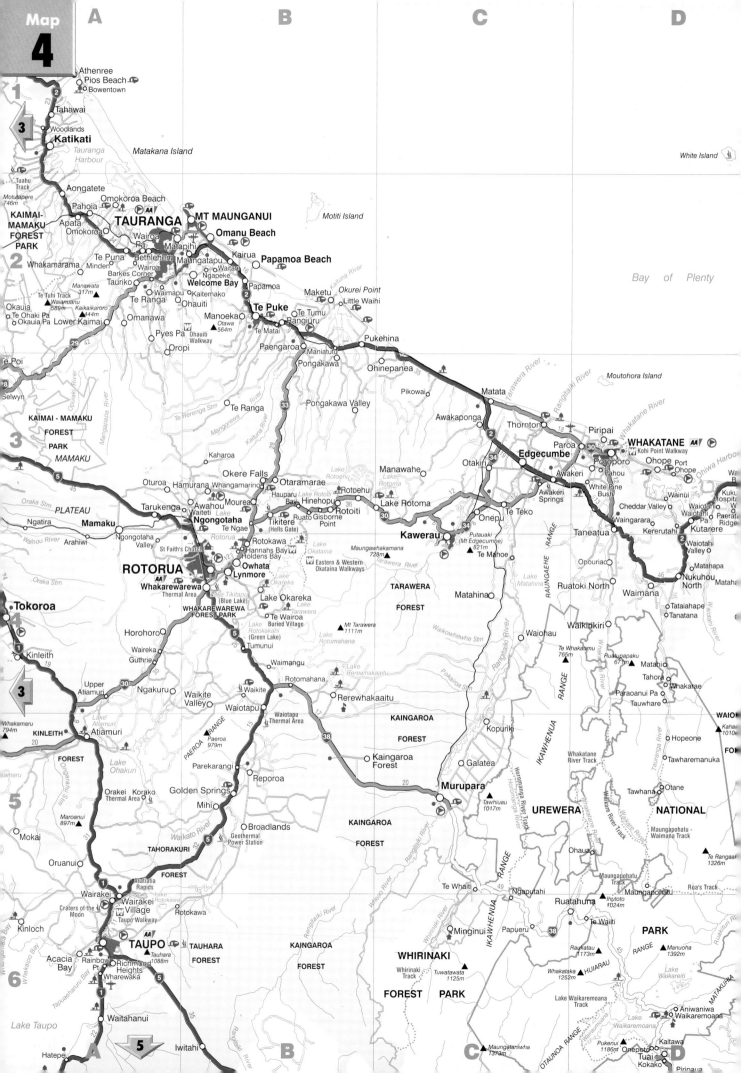

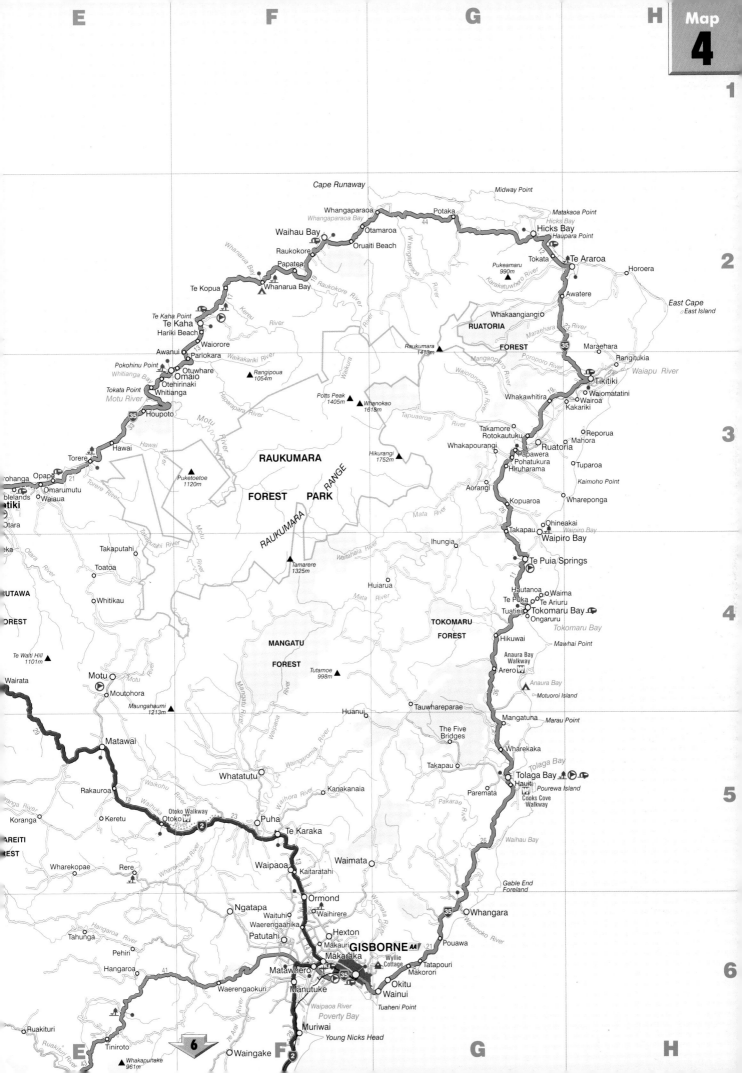

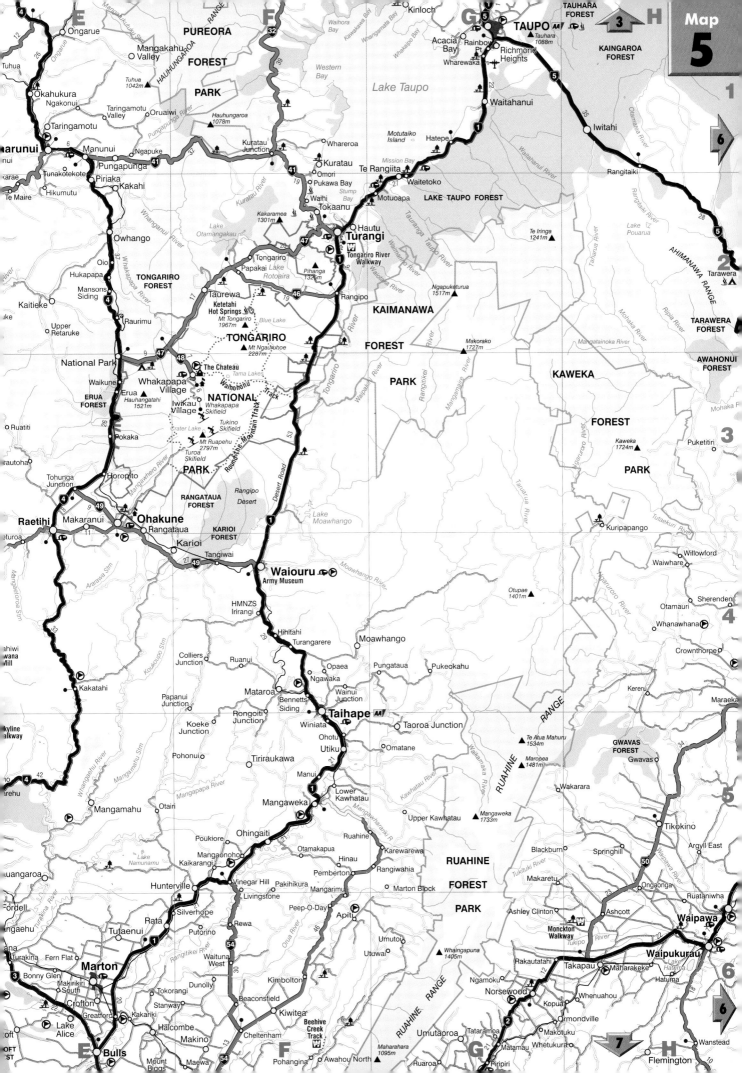

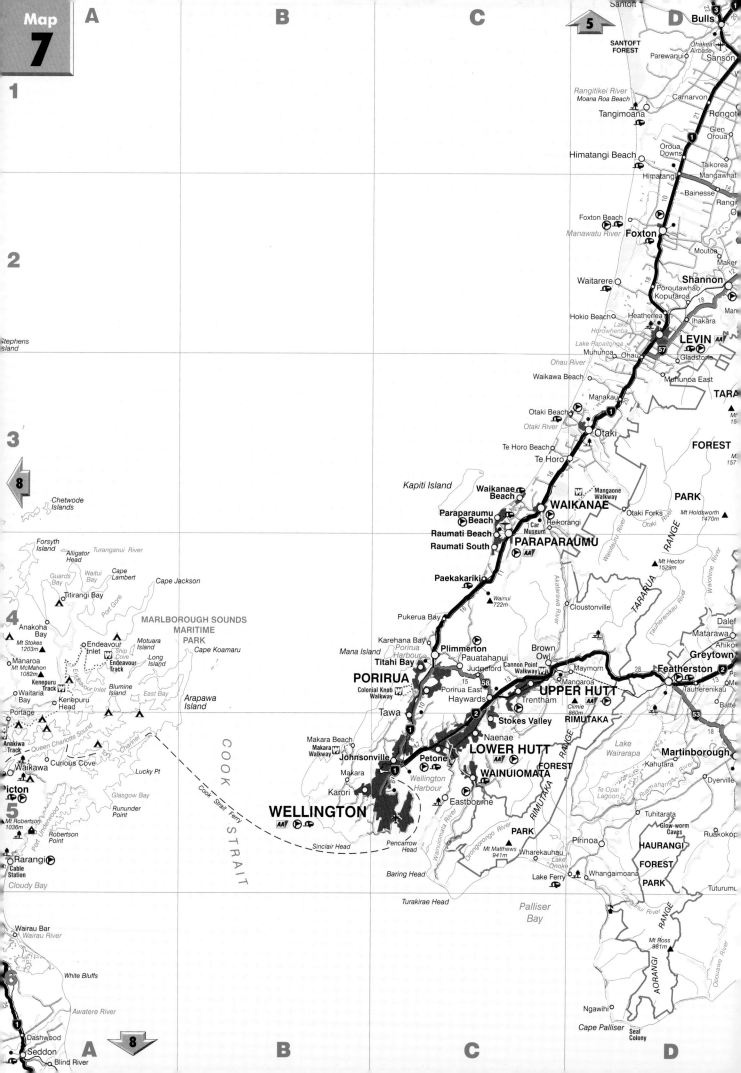

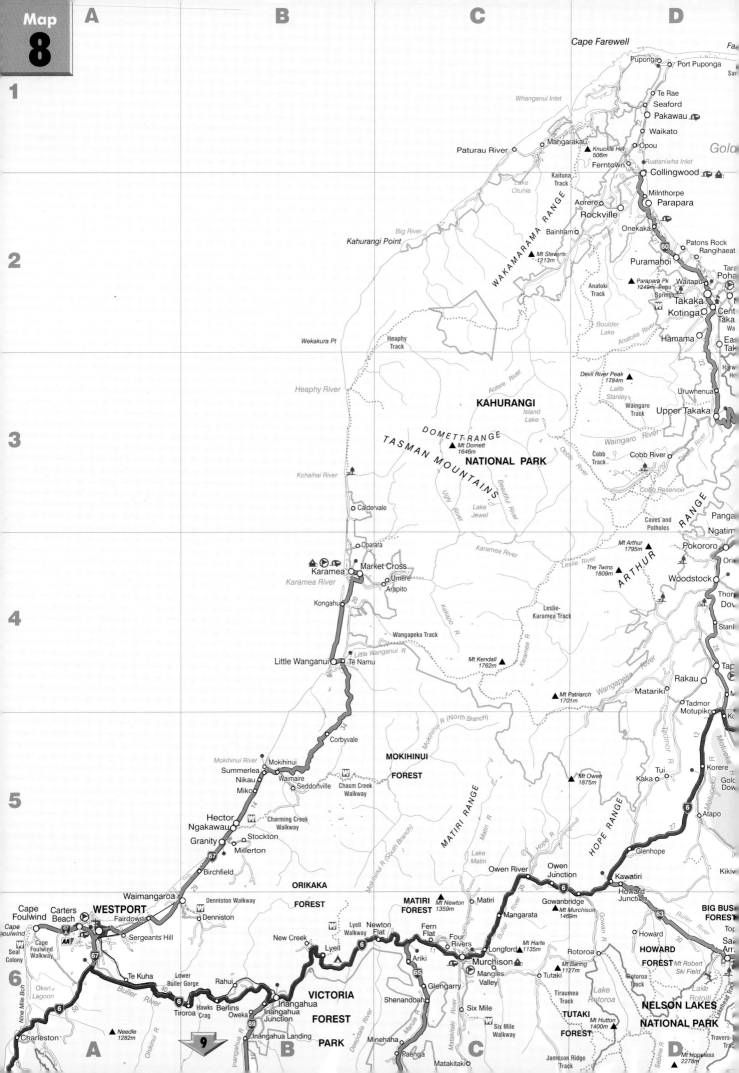

Map
8

A   B   C   D

1

2

3

4

5

6

Cape Farewell

Puponga
Port Puponga
Te Rae
Seaford
Pakawau
Waikato
Opou
Mangarakau
Knuckle Hill
506m
Ferntown
Collingwood
Milnthorpe
Parapara
Patons Rock
Rangihaeat
Puramahoi
Takaka
Kotinga
Cent
Taka
Hamama
Eas
Tak

Whanganui Inlet

Paturau River

Lake
Otuhie

WAKAMARAMA RANGE

Mt Stevens
1213m

Aorere
Rockville
Bainham

Kaituna
Track

Anatoki
Track

Ruataniwha Inlet

Gold

Parapara Pk
1249m Pupu
Spring

Waitapu
Poha

Uruwhenua

Upper Takaka

Harw
Ho

Kahurangi Point

Big River

Wekakura Pt

Heaphy
Track

Heaphy River

Kohaihai River

KAHURANGI

DOMETT RANGE

TASMAN MOUNTAINS

Mt Domett
1646m

NATIONAL PARK

Island
Lake

Lake
Jewel

Devil River Peak
1784m
Lake
Stanley

Waingaro
Track

Cobb
Track

Cobb River

Cobb Reservoir

Waingaro River

ARTHUR   RANGE

Panga
Ngatim

Pokororo

Ori

Woodstock

Thor
Dov

Stanl

Tap

Rakau

Matariki

Tadmor
Motupiko

Ko

Korere
Gol
Dow

Caldervale

Oparara

Karamea
Market Cross
Umere
Arapito

Kongahu

Karamea River

Mt Arthur
1795m

The Twins
1809m

Leslie River

Karamea River

Leslie-
Karamea Track

Wangapeka Track

Little Wanganui
Te Namu

Little Wanganui R

Kekaho R

Mt Kendall
1762m

Mt Patriarch
1701m

Wangapeka River

Corbyvale

Mokihinui River

Summerlea
Nikau
Miko
Mokihinui
Waimaire
Seddonville

Chasm Creek
Walkway

MOKIHINUI

FOREST

Mokihinui R (North Branch)

MATIRI RANGE

Mt Owen
1875m

Tui

Kaka

HOPE RANGE

Atapo

Hector
Ngakawau
Granity

Charming Creek
Walkway

Stockton
Millerton

Birchfield

Mokihinui R (South Branch)

Lake
Matiri

Matiri R

Hope R

Owen River

Owen
Junction

Glenhope

Kawatiri

Howard
Junction

Waimangaroa

ORIKAKA

Denniston Walkway

FOREST

Denniston

MATIRI
FOREST

Mt Newton
1359m

Matiri

Mangarata

Gowanbridge
Mt Murchison
1469m

Howard

63

BIG BUS
FOREST

Top

Sar
Ar

HOWARD

FOREST Mt Robert
Ski Field

Cape
Foulwind
Carters
Beach

WESTPORT

Fairdown

Sergeants Hill

New Creek

Lyell
Walkway

Newton
Flat

Fern
Flat

Four
Rivers

Longford

Mt Harte
1135m

Rotoroa

Mt Baring
1127m

Cape
Foulwind

Seal
Colony

Cape
Foulwind
Walkway

AA

Te Kuha

Lower
Buller Gorge

Rahui

Lyell

Ariki

Murchison

Mangles
Valley

Tutaki

Rotoroa
Track

Lake
Rotoroa

NELSON LAKES

Okari
Lagoon

Nine Mile Bch

Charleston

Buller River

Needle
1282m

Tiroroa

Hawks
Crag

Berlins
Oweka

Inangahua
Junction

Inangahua

VICTORIA

FOREST

PARK

Inangahua Landing

Glengarry

Shenandoah

Six Mile

Deepdale River

Six Mile
Walkway

Minehaha

Paenga

Matakitaki

Mangles River

Matakitaki River

TUTAKI

FOREST

Mt Hutton
1400m

Jameson Ridge

NATIONAL PARK

Travers

Mt Hopeless
2278m

9

A   B   C   D

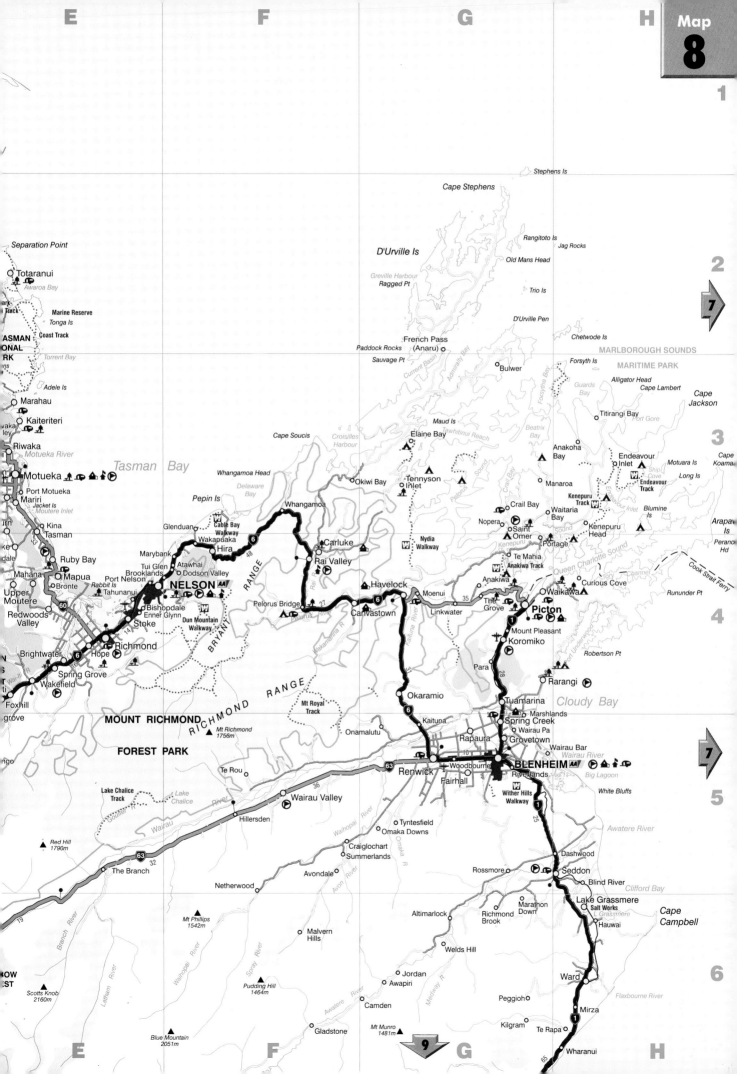

Map labels:

E F G H

1

Stephens Is
Cape Stephens

Separation Point
Rangitoto Is
Jag Rocks

Totaranui
Awaroa Bay
D'Urville Is
Old Mans Head

2

7

Park Track
Marine Reserve
Tonga Is
Greville Harbour
Ragged Pt
Trio Is

TASMAN NATIONAL PARK
Coast Track
D'Urville Pen
Chetwode Is

Torrent Bay
French Pass (Anaru)
Paddock Rocks
Bulwer
Forsyth Is
MARLBOROUGH SOUNDS

Adele Is
Sauvage Pt
Current Basin
Guards Bay
MARITIME PARK

Alligator Head
Cape Lambert

Marahau
Maud Is
Titirangi Bay
Cape Jackson

Kaiteriteri
Cape Soucis
Croisilles Harbour
Tawhitinui Reach
Elaine Bay
Beatrix Bay
Anakoha Bay
Port Gore
Endeavour Inlet
Motuara Is
Cape Koamaru

3

Riwaka
Motueka River
Whangamoa Head
Delaware Bay
Okiwi Bay
Tennyson Inlet
Pelorus Sound
Manaroa
Endeavour Track
Long Is
Arapawa Is

Tasman Bay
Pepin Is
Whangamoa
Crail Bay
Kenepuru Track
Blumine Is
Perano Hd

Motueka
Port Motueka
Glenduan
Cable Bay Walkway
Nopera
Saint Omer
Waitaria Bay
Kenepuru Head

Mariri
Jacket Is
Moutere Inlet
Wakapuaka
Hira
Carluke
Nydia Walkway
Te Mahia
Portage
Runder Pt

Kina
Tasman
Marybank
Rai Valley
Anakiwa Track
Curious Cove

Ruby Bay
Atawhai
Dodson Valley
RANGE
Anakiwa
Waikawa

Mahana
Mapua
Brooklands
Tui Glen
Pelorus Bridge
Havelock
Moenui
The Grove
Picton
4

Bronte
Port Nelson
Dun Mountain Walkway
Canvastown
Linkwater
Mount Pleasant

Upper Moutere
NELSON
Bishopdale
Enner Glynn
Pelorus River
35
Koromiko

Redwoods Valley
Stoke
BRYANT
Robertson Pt

Tahunanui
Okaramio
Para
Rarangi

Brightwater
Hope
Richmond
RANGE
Kaituna
Tuamarina
Cloudy Bay

Spring Grove
Mt Royal Track
6
Marshlands

Wakefield
Onamalutu
Spring Creek
Wairau Pa

Foxhill
MOUNT RICHMOND
RICHMOND
Mt Richmond 1756m
Rapaura
Grovetown

grove
FOREST PARK
Te Rou
Renwick
Woodbourne
BLENHEIM
Wairau Bar
Big Lagoon

63
Fairhall
Riverlands

Lake Chalice Track
Lake Chalice
Wairau Valley
36
Wither Hills Walkway
White Bluffs

5

Red Hill 1790m
Hillersden
Tyntesfield
Omaka Downs
Dashwood

63 32
The Branch
Craiglochart
Summerlands
Rossmore
Seddon
Blind River

Netherwood
Avondale
Lake Grassmere
Salt Works
Clifford Bay

Mt Phillips 1542m
Malvern Hills
Altimarlock
Richmond Brook
Marathon Down
Hauwai
Cape Campbell

6

Scotts Knob 2160m
Pudding Hill 1464m
Jordan
Awapiri
Welds Hill
Peggioh
Ward

Blue Mountain 2051m
Camden
Mt Munro 1481m
Gladstone
Kilgram
Te Rapa
Mirza

9
Wharanui
65

E F G H

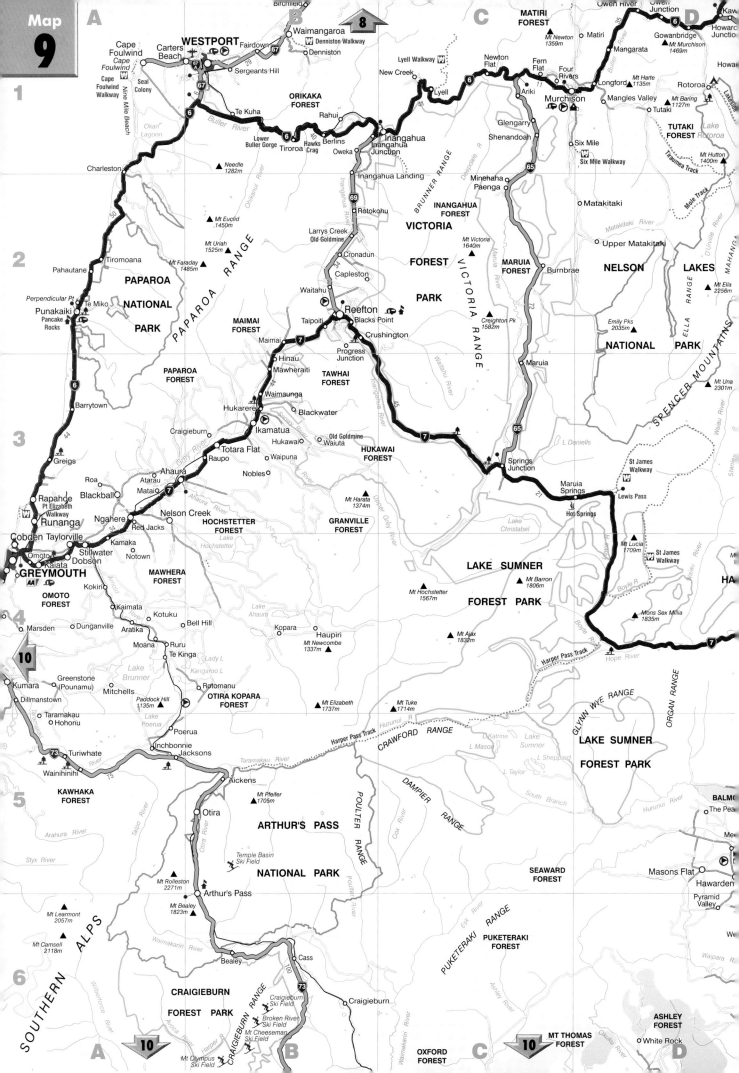

Map
9

E   F   G   8   H

Kikiwa
The Branch
63   32
Avondale
Rossmore   Seddon
Netherwood
Marathon Down
Altimarlock   Richmond Brook
Wairau River
Tophouse
Mt Phillips 1542m
Malvern Hills
Welds Hill
Flaxbourne River

St Arnaud
St Arnaud 1683m
RAINBOW FOREST
Jordan
Ward
1
Lake Rotoiti
Scotts Knob 2160m
Pudding Hill 1464m
Awapiri
Peggioh
Mirza
Lakehead Track
Camden
Kilgram
Te Rapa
Rainbow Valley Ski Field
Blue Mountain 2051m
Gladstone
Mt Munro 1481m
Wharanui
Peak
Sabine Track
RAGLAN RANGE
65

Mt Gladstone 2371m
Langridge
Middlehurst
Tapuae-o-Uenuku 2885m
Kekerengu
2
Mt Weld 2118m
Severn 2027m
Molesworth
INLAND KAIKOURA RANGE
RANGE
Mt Union 2287m
Parikawa
BODDINGTON RANGE
Saxton River
Mt Major 2271m
Awatere River
Clarence River

Mt Tarndale 1774m
Turks Head 1959m
St Bernard 2256m
Clarence
Clarence River
L McRea
42

Mt Sebastopol 2013m
Alma River
Clarence River
SEAWARD KAIKOURA RANGE
Te ao Whekere 2596m
Acheron River
Dillon R
Rakautara
3
Mangamaunu
Mt Fyffe 1602m
Hapuku
1
Mt Fyffe
Charwell River
Kaikoura
Seal Colony & Whale Watching
Kowhai
Puketa
Kaikoura Peninsula
South Bay
Kaikoura Peninsula Walkway

Mt Tinline 1747m
Goose Bay
4
HANMER RANGE
Mt Lyford Ski Field
14
REST PARK
AMURI RANGE
Oaro
9   7A
Hanmer Springs
RANGE
78
16
Hundalee
Claverley
1
Conway Flat
Fernlehurst
Conway River
Waiau River
Waiau
30
Hawkswood
17
Rotherham
Waiau River
Parnassus
70
Phoebe
Spotswood
5
Culverden
Leamington
Caverhill
22
Waiau River
REST
16
Cheviot
ahau oral
Nonoti
Gore Bay
Beckenham Hills
Port Robinson Track
Domett
Port Robinson
Hurunui Mouth
Tormore
Hurunui River
27
Blythe Valley
Scargill
Davaar
6
Motunau
Spye
Omihi
22
Waipara
Motunau Beach
Motunau Is
asnevin
berley
Amberley Beach
eithfield
E   F   G   H

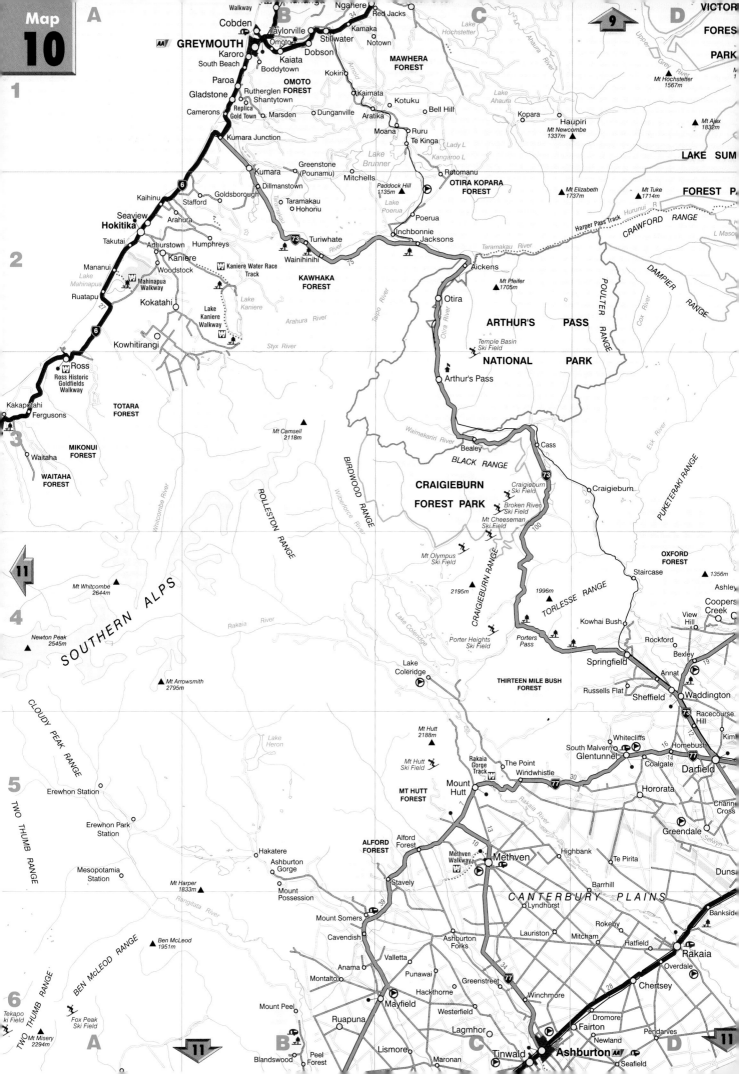

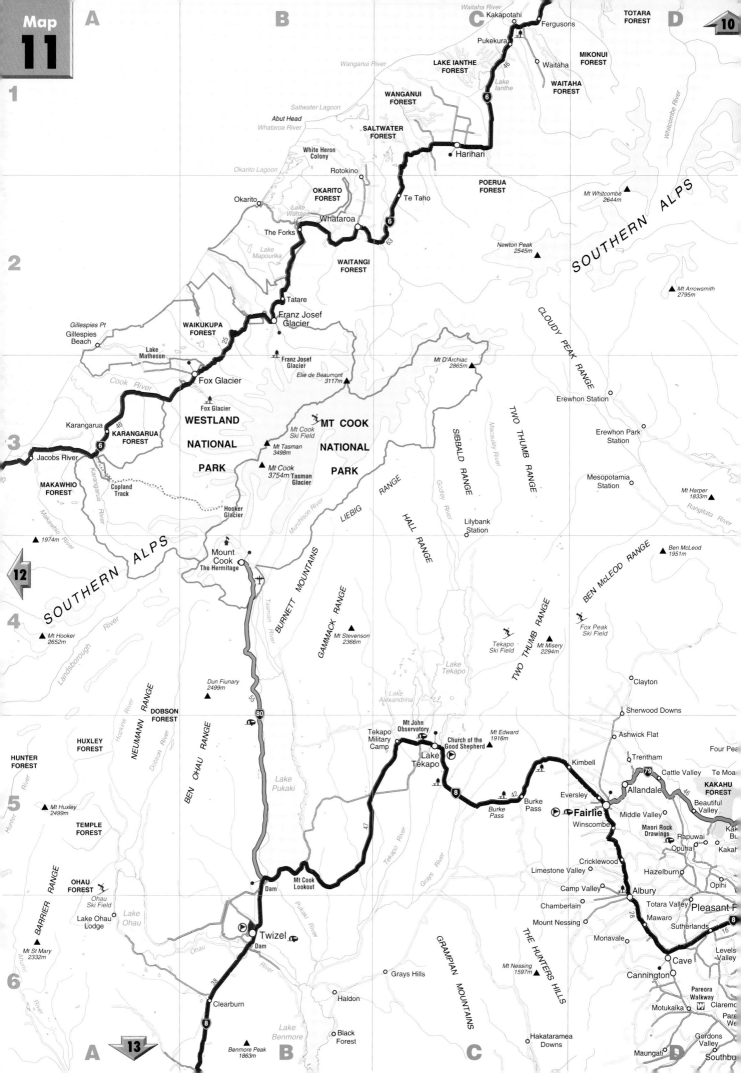

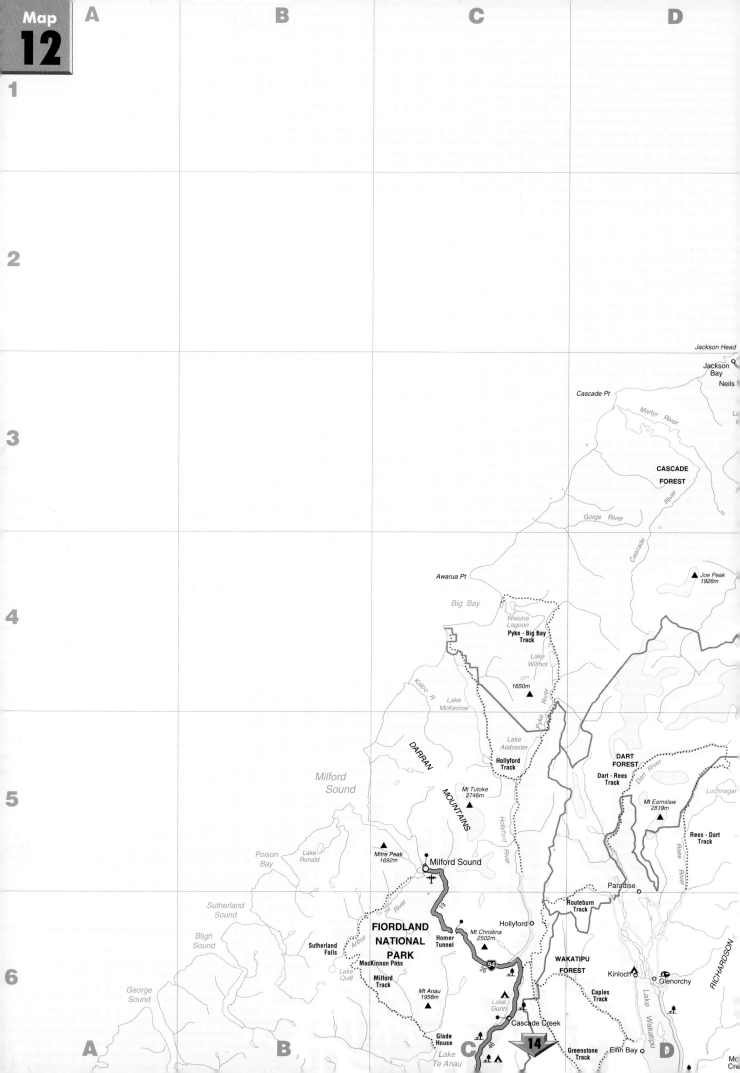

Map
12

A   B   C   D

1

2

Jackson Head

Jackson
Bay
Neils

Cascade Pt

Martyr River

3   CASCADE
                                               FOREST

Gorge River

Cascade

Awarua Pt   ▲ Joe Peak
                                                 1926m

Big Bay

Waiuna
Lagoon
**Pyke - Big Bay
Track**

4

*Lake
Wilmot*

Kaipo R

1650m
▲

*Lake
McKerrow*

Pyke River

DART
FOREST

*Lake
Alabaster*

Dart - Rees
Track

Dart River

DARRAN   Hollyford
                Track

*Milford
Sound*

▲ Mt Tutoke
  2746m

MOUNTAINS

Hollyford

▲ Mt Earnslaw
  2819m

Lochnagar

5

River

Rees - Dart
Track

*Poison
Bay*   *Lake
            Ronald*

▲ Mitre Peak
  1692m   ○ Milford Sound

*Rees
River*

RICHARDSON

*Sutherland
Sound*

River

19

Paradise ○

*Bligh
Sound*

**FIORDLAND
NATIONAL
PARK**

• Mt Christina
  2502m

Hollyford ○

Routeburn
Track

Sutherland
Falls

Homer
Tunnel

94

WAKATIPU
FOREST

Kinloch ▲

Glenorchy ○

6   *George
           Sound*

MacKinnon Pass

*Lake
Quill*   Milford
          Track

26

▲ Mt Anau
  1958m

Caples
Track

*Lake
Wakatipu*

*Lake
Gunn*

Cascade Creek ○

⬇ 14

Glade
House

46

Greenstone
Track

Elfin Bay ○

*Lake
Te Anau*

A   B   C   D

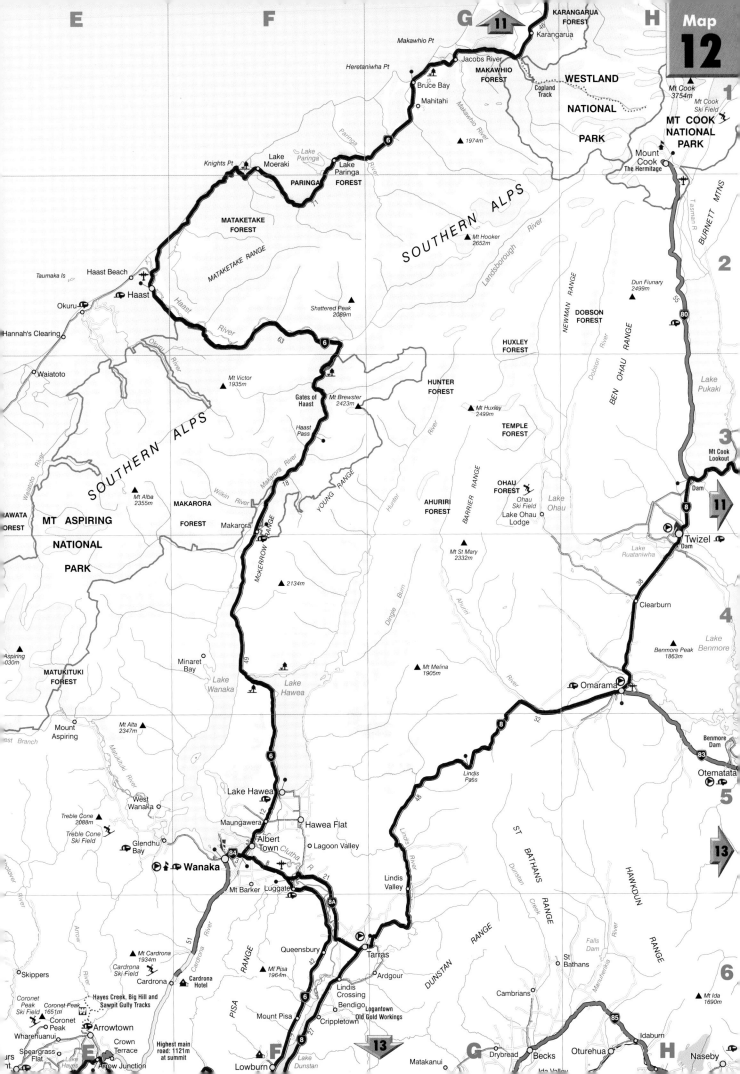

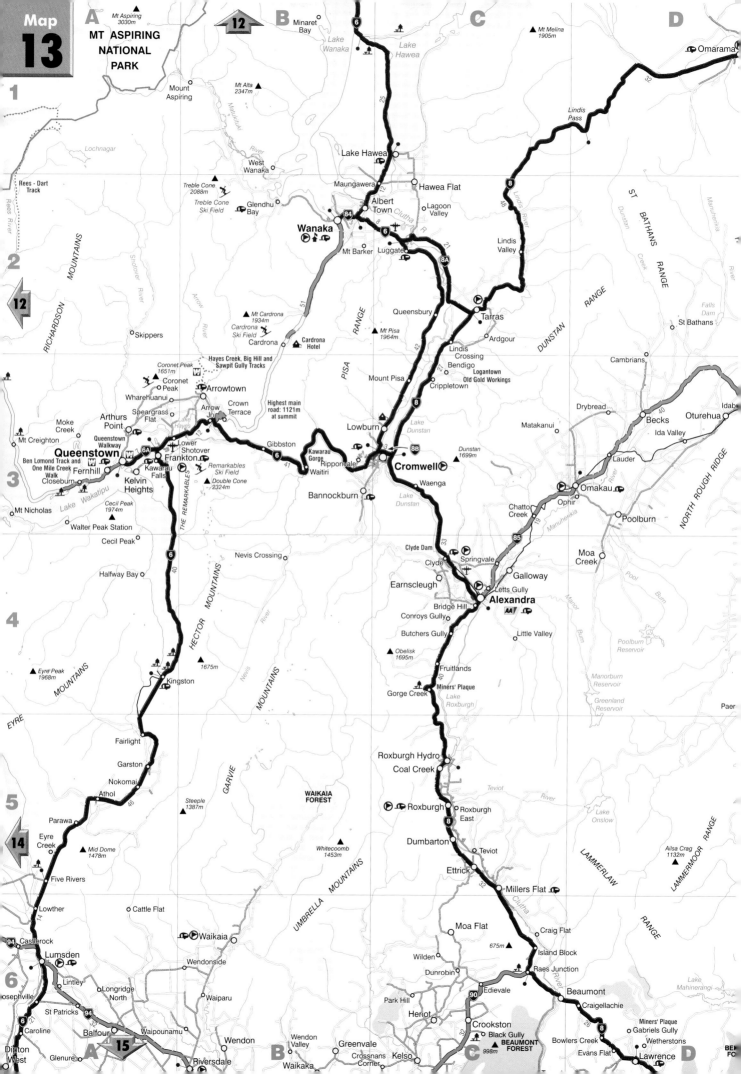

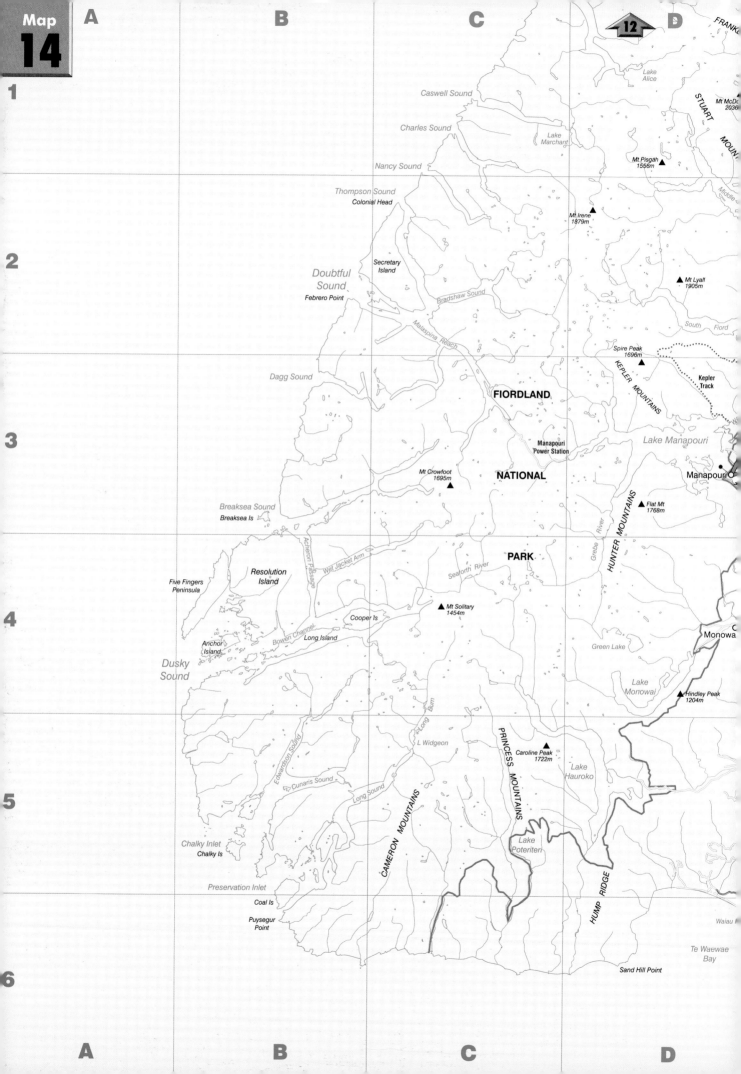

Map
14

A   B   C   D

1

2

3

4

5

6

12

FRANK

Lake
Alice

Caswell Sound

Charles Sound

Nancy Sound

Thompson Sound
Colonial Head

Doubtful
Sound

Secretary
Island

Febrero Point

Bradshaw Sound

Malaspina Reach

Dagg Sound

FIORDLAND

Manapouri
Power Station

NATIONAL

Mt Crowfoot
1695m

Breaksea Sound
Breaksea Is

Acheron Passage

Wet Jacket Arm

Seaforth River

PARK

Resolution
Island

Five Fingers
Peninsula

Cooper Is

Bowen Channel   Long Island

Mt Solitary
1454m

Anchor
Island

Dusky
Sound

Edwardson Sound

Cunaris Sound

Long Sound

Long Burn

L Widgeon

Chalky Inlet
Chalky Is

Preservation Inlet

Coal Is

Puysegur
Point

CAMERON MOUNTAINS

PRINCESS MOUNTAINS

Caroline Peak
1722m

Lake
Hauroko

Lake
Poteriteri

HUMP RIDGE

STUART MOUN

Mt McDo
2036

Mt Pisgah
1556m

Mt Irene
1879m

Mt Lyall
1905m

Middle

South Fiord

Spire Peak
1696m

KEPLER MOUNTAINS

Kepler
Track

Lake Manapouri

Manapouri

Flat Mt
1768m

Grebe River

HUNTER MOUNTAINS

Monowa

Green Lake

Lake
Monowai

Hindley Peak
1204m

Waiau

Te Waewae
Bay

Sand Hill Point

A   B   C   D

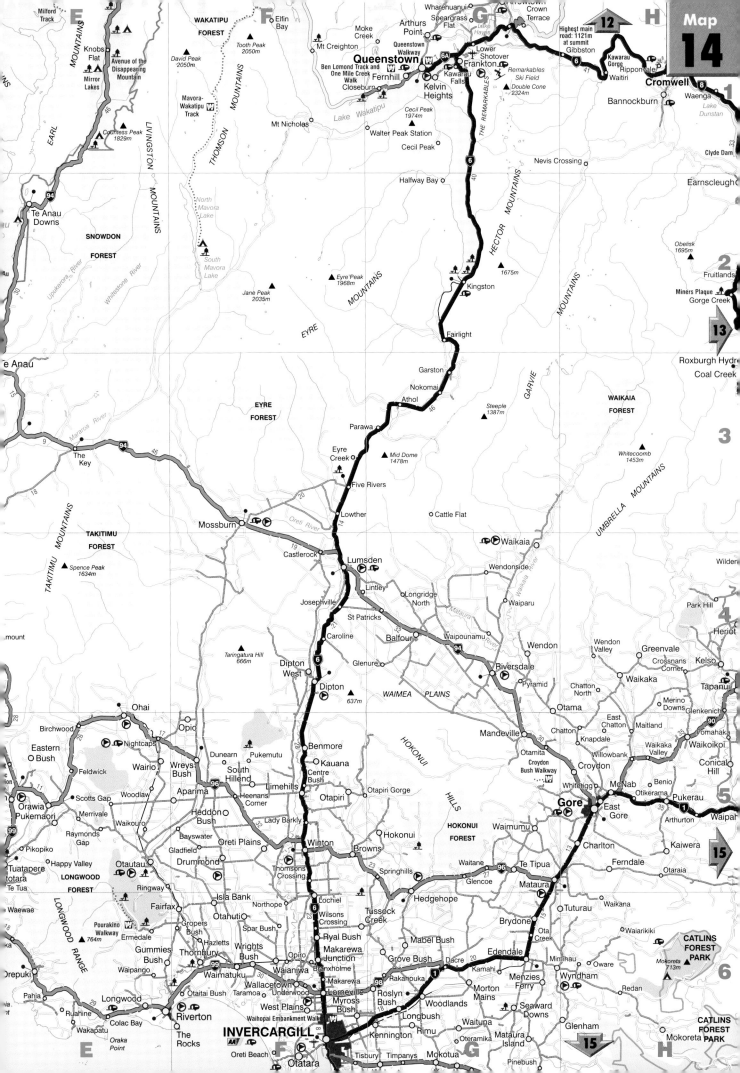

Map
15

A · B · C · D

EYRE FOREST

Garston
Nokomai
Athol
46
Parawa
Eyre Creek
Mid Dome 1478m
Five Rivers
Lowther
Cattle Flat
14

13

Steeple 1387m

Nevis River

Roxburgh H
Coal Cre

WAIKAIA FOREST
Rox

UMBRELLA MOUNTAINS

Whitecoomb 1453m

Dum
Wi

14

TAKITIMU MOUNTAINS
TAKITIMU FOREST
Spence Peak 1634m

9
94
46
The Key
11
18
35

Mossburn
20
19
Castlerock
Lumsden
Lintley
Longridge North
Josephville
St Patricks
Caroline
Balfour
Waipounamu
Wendon
Greenvale
Kelso
Tapar
90
Waikoikoi
Conica Hill

21
32
94
Waikaia
Wendonside
Waiparu
Mataura River
Waikaka River

Wendon Valley
Crossnans Corner
Waikaka
Merino Downs
Glenkenich

Dipton West
Glenure
Riversdale
Pyramid
Otama
Chatton North
Chatton
Maitland
6
WAIMEA PLAINS
Mandeville
30
Knapdale
East Chatton
Waikaka Valley
Willowbank

Dipton
637m
Otamita
Croydon Bush Walkway
Croydon
Whiterigg
McNab
Benio
Otikerama
Pukerau
Wa

TARINGATURA HILL 666m

Benmore
Kauana
Centre Bush
Otapiri
Otapiri Gorge
HOKONUI
HILLS
HOKONUI FOREST
Waimumu
Gore
East Gore
Arthurton
35
1

Ohai
Opio
Dunearn
Pukemutu
Limehills
Heenans Corner
Hokonui
Charlton
Ferndale
Kaiwera
Otaraia

Birchwood
Nightcaps
Wairio
Wreys Bush
South Hillend
Lady Barkly
Winton
Browns
Springhills
96
Waitane
Glencoe
Te Tipua
Mataura
Tuturau
Waikana

Eastern Bush
17
26
Feldwick
Aparima
Heddon Bush
Bayswater
Gladfield
Drummond
Oreti Plains
Thompsons Crossing
23
Hedgehope
13
Brydone
Ota Creek
Waiarikiki
CATLINS FOREST PARK
713m
Mokoreta

Otahu Flat
Historic Suspension Bridge
Clifden
Orawia
Pukemaori
Scotts Gap
Merrivale
Waikouro
Raymonds Gap
Woodlaw
Ringway
Isla Bank
Northope
Spar Bush
Wilsons Crossing
6
Tussock Creek
Mabel Bush
20
Edendale
5
Mimihau
Oware
Wyndham
Redan
Mokoreta

12
99
11
Pikopiko
Happy Valley
Otautau
Fairfax
Gropers Bush
Hazletts
Ryal Bush
Makarewa Junction
Grove Bush
98
Dacre
Kamahi
Menzies Ferry
Glenham

Tuatapere
Te Tua
LONGWOOD FOREST
Pourakino Walkway 764m
Ermedale
Gummies Bush
Thornbury
Wrights Bush
Branxholme
Rakahouka
1
Morton Mains
Seaward Downs
Mataura Island

Te Waewae
18
LONGWOOD RANGE
Waipango
99
30
Waimatuku
Waianiwa
Waiatown
Makarewa
Underwood
Lorneville
Myross Bush
Roslyn Bush
Woodlands
Waituna
Glenham

Waihoaka
Orepuki
Longwood
29
Otaitai Bush
Taramoa
West Plains
Longbush
Waituna
Oteramika
Mokoreta

Pahia Point
Pahia
Ruahine
Colac Bay
Riverton
The Rocks
Waihopai Embankment Walk
INVERCARGILL
AA
Otatara
Clifton
Tisbury
Timpanys
Kennington
Rimu
Mokotua
Ashers
46
Pinebush
Titiroa
Te Peka
Fortification
Waikawa

14
Wakapatu
Oraka Point
Oreti Beach
Waimatua
Kapuka
Gorge Road
Kapuka South
Waimahaka
Quarry Hills
28
Waikawa

Centre Island
Clifton
Woodend
Awarua
1
30
Fortrose
Tokanui
Niagara
Progre
Valle
CAT

Greenhills
Greenpoint
Bluff
Bluff Harbour
Aluminium Smelter
Awarua Bay
Waituna Lagoon
Mataura R
Haldane
Otara
Waikawa
Slope Point
Porpoise Bay

FOVEAUX

Foveaux Walkway
Tiwai Point
Dog Island
Toetoes Bay
Waipapa Point
Petrified Forest

STRAIT

Ruapuke Island

Codfish Island

Stewart Island

6

Halfmoon Bay
Paterson Inlet

A · B · C · D

Map
15

13

E F G H

Puketapu
Wairunga
Flag Swamp
Goodwood
Hawkesbury Bush
Tumai
Middlemarch
Waikouaiti

Sutton

Merton
Karitane

Mount Stoker
Puketeraki

87

Seacliff
Omimi

Shannon

Warrington
Silverpeaks
Evansdale
Doctors Pt
Michies Crossing
Purakanui
Clarks Junction
Hindon
Waitati
Long Beach
52
Upper Waitati
Osborne
Heyward Pt
Lee
Flat
Swampy Ridge
Walkway
Miniwaka
Albatross Colony
Aramoana
Lee Stream
Pigeon Flat
Mt Cargill
Swamp
Wharf
Upper
Otakou
Flat
Junction
North
Flagstaff
Harwood
Taieri
Walkway
Port Chalmers
Wylies
Woodside
Crossing
Glenleith
Portobello
Broad Bay
Outram
Janefield
Macandrew
Hoopers Inlet
13
Wingatu
Green
Bay
Sandymount
Riverside
Mosgiel
Is
88
Maungatua
East Taieri
Pukehiki
895m ▲
Allanton
Owhiro
Highcliff
Waipori Falls
Momona
DUNEDIN
Otago Peninsula
Fairfield
BERWICK
Otokia
Saddle
Waldronville
FOREST
Hill
Berwick
25
Scroggs
Hill
Ocean View
Brighton

Henley

Titri
Lake
Waihola
Kuri Bush
Waihola
Taieri River
Taieri Mouth
Circle
Hill
17
Clarendon
Table Hill
Kapiti
Taieri Beach
Manuka Creek
Milburn
Akatore
Mount Stuart
33
Round Hill
Glenore
Hélensbrook
Glenledi
Pukekoma
OTAGO
COAST
FOREST
Adams Flat
Milton
Brooklands
Awamangu
Clarksville
McNally Track
Hillend
Tokoiti
Crichton
Toko Mouth
Moneymore
Lovells Flat
Stony
Creek
1
Benhar
Balclutha
Stirling
Finegand
Wangaloa
Kaitangata
Otanomomo
Summer Hill
Waitepeka
Puerua
Paretai
Clutha River
Romahapa
Port Molyneux
Kaka
Molyneux
Point
Bay
Glenomaru
Ahuriri
Flat
Hays Gap
Tirohanga
Katea
Otekura
Kaimataitai
Owaka Valley
Nugget
Point
Owaka
Tawanui
Houipapa
Newhaven
Puketiro
Hinahina
Pounawea
38
Ratanui
Tarara
Caberfeidh
Purakaunui
Kahuika
Purakauiti
Maclennan
35
Papatowai

Tautuku
Peninsula

Chaslands
Mistake

E F G H

1
2
3
4
5
6

Index of New Zealand Place Names

The place name *Acacia Bay* can be found on **Map 3** (map number in top outside corner)
and within a square formed by the **co-ordinates E6**

Names on town plans are not included in this index

Map Number>3/E6<Co-ordinate

Map Number/Co-ordinate

Blackmount

Blackmount 14D4
Blackpool 2E5
Blacks Point 9B2
Blackwater 9B3
Blairlogie 7F4
Blandswood 11E4
Blenheim 8G5
Blind River 8H5
Blue Cliffs 13G1
Bluff 15B5
Blythe Valley 9F5
Boddytown 10B1
Bombay 2E6
Bonny Glen 5E6
Bortons 13F2
Bowentown 3E2
Bowlers Creek 13D6
Braeburn 8E3
Braigh 2C1
Branxholme 15B4
Bridge Hill 13C4
Bridge Pa 6E5
Brighton 15G2
Brightwater 8E4
Brixton 5B2
Broad Bay 13F6
Broad Gully 13G2
Broadfield 10E5
Broadlands 3F6
Broadwood 1D4
Bronte 8E4
Brookby 2E5
Brooklands 8E4
Brooklands 10F4
Brooklands 15F3
Brooklyn 8E3
Brookside 10E6
Brown Owl 7C4
Browns 15B3
Browns Beach 11E6
Bruce Bay 12G1
Brunswick 5D5
Bruntwood 3C3
Brydone 15C4
Brynavon 1G6
Brynderwyn 2C2
Buckland 2E6
Buckland 3D3
Bulls 5E6
Bulwer 8G3
Bunnythorpe 7E1
Burke Pass 11C5
Burnbrae 9C2
Burnham 10E5
Bushey 13F5
Butchers Gully 13C4

C

Caberfeidh 15E5
Cable Bay 1D3
Caldervale 8B3
Cambrians 13D2
Cambridge 3D3
Camden Stn 9G1
Camerons 10B1
Camp Valley 11D5
Cannington 11D6
Canvastown 8F4
Cape Foulwind 8A6
Cape Reinga 1A1
Cappleston 9B2
Cardiff 5B3
Cardrona 13B2
Carew 11E4
Carleton 10E4
Carluke 8F4
Carnarvon 7D1
Caroline 13A6
Carrington 7E4
Carters Beach 8A6
Carterton 7E4
Cascade Creek 12C6
Cass 9B6
Castlecliff 5D5
Castlehill 7F3
Castlepoint 7F4
Castlerock 15B2
Cattle Creek 13F1
Cattle Flat 13A6
Cattle Valley 11D5
Cave 11D6
Cavendish 10B6
Caverhill 9F5
Cecil Peak 13A4
Central Takaka 8D2
Centre Bush 15B3
Chamberlain 11D6
Chaneys 10F5
Charing Cross 10D5
Charleston 8A6
Charlton 15D3
Charteris Bay 10F5
Chaslands 15E5
Chatto Creek 13C3
Chatton 15D3
Chatton North 15D2
Cheddar Valley 3H4
Cheltenham 5F6
Chertsey 10D6
Chesterfield 10B1
Cheviot 9F5
Chorlton 10G5
Christchurch 10F5
Churchill 3B1

Circle Hill 15F3
Clandeboye 11E5
Claremont 11D6
Clarence 9H2
Clarendon 15F3
Clareville 7E4
Claris 2F2
Clarkeville 10F4
Clarks Beach 2D6
Clarks Flat 15E2
Clarks Junction 13E6
Clarksville 15F3
Claverley 9F4
Clayton 11D4
Clearburn 11B6
Clevedon 2E5
Clifden 15A3
Clifton 6F4
Clifton 8D2
Clifton 15B5
Clifton 15E3
Clinton 15E3
Clive 6E4
Closeburn 13A3
Cloustonville 7C4
Clyde 13C4
Clydevale 15E3
Coal Creek 13C5
Coalgate 10D5
Coatesville 2D4
Cobb River 8D3
Cobden 10B1
Colac Bay 15A4
Coldstream 10F4
Coldstream 11E5
Colliers Junction 5F4
Collingwood 8D2
Colville 2F4
Colyton 7E1
Conical Hill 15D3
Conroys Gully 13C4
Conway Flat 9F4
Cooks Beach 2G5
Coonoor 7F2
Coopers Beach 1D3
Coopers Creek 10D4
Cooptown 10F6
Corbyvale 8B5
Cornwallis 2D5
Coroglen 2G5
Coromandel 2F4
Coronet Peak 13A3
Corriedale 13F3
Courtney 10E5
Coutts Island 10F5
Craig Flat 13C6
Craigellachie 13D6

Dunback

Craigieburn 9B3
Craigieburn 9B6
Craiglochart 8F5
Crail Bay 8G3
Crichton 15F3
Cricklewood 11D5
Crippletown 13C3
Croften 5E6
Cromwell 13C3
Cronadun 9B2
Crookston 13C6
Crossans Corner 15D2
Crown Terrace 13B3
Crownthorpe 6D4
Croydon 15D3
Crushington 9B2
Culverden 9E5
Curious Cove 8H4
Cust 10E4
Cuthill 2D4

D

Dacre 15C4
Dairy Flat 2D4
Dalefield 7D4
Dannevirke 7F1
Danseys Pass 13F3
Darfield 10D5
Dargaville 2B1
Dashwood 8H5
Davaar 9E5
Dawson Falls 5B3
Deborah 13G3
Deep Creek 13G2
Denniston 8B6
Diamond Harbour 10F5
Diggers Valley 1C4
Dillmanstown 10B2
Dipton 15B2
Dipton West 15B2
Dobson 9A4
Doctors Point 13F6
Dodson Valley 8F4
Dome Valley 2D3
Domett 9F5
Donnellys Crossing 1D6
Douglas 5C3
Douglas 13G2
Dovedale 8D4
Doyleston 10E6
Dreyers Rock 7E3
Dromore 10D6
Drummond 15B3
Drury 2E6
Drybread 13D3
Dumbarton 13C5
Dunback 13F4

101

Dunearn

Hangaroa

Hangatiki

Kaimataitai

Kaimaumau

Map Number/Co-ordinate

Laingholm

Laingholm	2D5
Lake Alice	5E6
Lake Coleridge	10C4
Lake Ferry	7D5
Lake Grassmere	8H6
Lake Hawea	13C1
Lake Hayes	13B3
Lake Moeraki	12F1
Lake Ohau Lodge	11A6
Lake Ohia	1C3
Lake Okareka	3F4
Lake Okareka	3F4
Lake Paringa	12F1
Lake Tekapo	11C5
Lake Waitaki	13E2
Lakeside	10E6
Langridge	9F2
Langs Beach	2D2
Lansdowne	10E5
Larrys Creek	9B2
Lauder	13D3
Lauriston	10C6
Lawrence	15E2
Leamington	3D3
Leamington	9F5
Le Bons Bay	10G6
Lee Flat	13E6
Lee Stream	13E6
Lees Valley	9C6
Leeston	10E6
Leigh	2D3
Leithfield	10F4
Leithfield Beach	10F4
Lepperton	5B2
Letts Gully	13C4
Levels	11E6
Levels Valley	11D6
Levin	7D2
Lichfield	3D4
Lilybank Stn	11C3
Limehills	15B3
Limestone Downs	3B1
Limestone Valley	11D5
Lincoln	10E5
Lindis Crossing	13C2
Lindis Valley	13C2
Linkwater	8G4
Lintley	13A6
Linton	7E2
Linton Military Camp	7E2
Lismore	10C6
Little Bay	2F4
Little Huia	2D5
Little Rakaia	10E6
Little River	10F6
Little Valley	13C4
Little Waihi	3F3

Little Wanganui	8B4
Livingstone	5F5
Livingstone	13F3
Loburn	10E4
Loburn North	10E4
Loch Norrie	2C4
Lochiel	15B4
Lochindorb	15E4
Long Bay	2D4
Long Beach	13F6
Longbeach	11F5
Longburn	7E1
Longbush	7E4
Longbush	15C4
Longford	8C6
Longlands	6E5
Longridge North	13A6
Longwood	15A4
Lorneville	15B4
Lovells Flat	15F3
Lowburn	13C3
Lowcliffe	11F5
Lower Hutt	7C5
Lower Kaimai	3E3
Lower Kawhatau	5F5
Lower Moutere	8E3
Lower Selwyn Huts	10E6
Lower Shotover	13A3
Lower Waihou	1C5
Lowther	13A6
Luggate	13C2
Lumsden	13A6
Lyalldale	13G1
Lyell	8B6
Lyndhurst	10C6
Lynmore	3F4
Lyttelton	10F5

M

Maata	5B3
Mabel Bush	15C4
Macandrew Bay	13F6
Mackaytown	3D1
Maclennan	15E5
Macraes Flat	13F4
Maeraweka	13F3
Maerewhenua	13F2
Maewa	7E1
Mahana	8E4
Mahanga	6H2
Maharahara	7F1
Maharakeke	5H6
Maheno	13G3
Mahia	6H2
Mahia Beach	6H2
Mahinepua	1E3
Mahitahi	12G1

Mahoe	5B3
Mahoenui	3B6
Mahora	4H3
Mahurangi	2D3
Mahurangi West	2D3
Mahuta	2B1
Mahuta	3C2
Maihiihi	3C4
Maimai	9B2
Maioro	3A1
Maioro Sands	3B1
Mairoa	3B5
Maitland	15D3
Makahu	5C3
Makakaho	5D4
Makakaho Junction	5D4
Makara	7B5
Makara Beach	7B5
Makaraka	4F6
Makaranui	5E3
Makarau	2C4
Makaretu	5G5
Makarowa	15B4
Makarewa Junction	15B4
Makarora	12F3
Makauri	4F6
Makerua	7D2
Maketu	3F3
Maketu Pa	3B4
Makikihi	13G1
Makino	5F6
Makirikiri	7F1
Makirikiri South	5E6
Makomako	3B3
Makomako	7E2
Makorori	4G6
Makotuku	5G6
Makuri	7F2
Malvern Hills	8F6
Mamaku	3E4
Mamaranui	1E6
Manaia	5B4
Manakau	7D3
Mananui	10A2
Manapouri	14D3
Manaroa	8G3
Manawahe	3G4
Manawaora	1F4
Manawaru	3D2
Mandeville	15C3
Mandeville North	10E4
Mangaeturoa	5E4
Mangahao	7E2
Mangaiti	3D2
Mangakahu Valley	5E1
Mangakino	3D5
Mangakura	2C3

Mansons Siding

Mangakuri Beach	6E6
Mangamahu	5E5
Mangamaire	7E2
Mangamaunu	9G3
Mangamingi	5C3
Mangamuka	1D4
Mangamuka Bridge	1D4
Mangamutu	7E2
Mangaonoho	5F5
Mangaorapa	7G1
Mangaore	7D2
Mangaorongo	3C4
Mangaotaki	3B5
Mangapa	1D4
Mangapai	1F6
Mangapakeha	7F4
Mangaparo	5D1
Mangapehi	3C6
Mangapiko	3C3
Mangapiko Valley	3C1
Mangarakau	8C1
Mangarata	8C6
Mangarawa	7F1
Mangarimu	5F5
Mangaroa	7C4
Mangatainoka	7F2
Mangataiore	1D4
Mangatangi	2E6
Mangatara	2B1
Mangataraire	1D5
Mangatarata	3C1
Mangatawhiri	2E6
Mangatea	3C5
Mangateparu	3D2
Mangateretere	6E4
Mangatoetoe	1D4
Mangatoi	3F3
Mangatoki	5B3
Mangatoro	7F1
Mangatu	1D6
Mangatuna	4G5
Mangatutu	3C4
Mangawara	3C2
Mangaweka	5F5
Mangawhai	2D2
Mangawhai Heads	2D2
Mangawhata	7D2
Mangawhero	1D5
Mangere	2D5
Mangles Valley	8C6
Mangonui	1D3
Mangorei	5B2
Mangungu	1D4
Maniatutu	3F3
Manly	2D4
Manoeka	3F3
Mansons Siding	5E2

105

Manui

Mount Barker

Mount Bruce

Mount Bruce	7E3
Mount Cargill	13F6
Mount Cook	11B4
Mount Hutt	10C5
Mount Maunganui	3F2
Mount Peel	10B6
Mount Pisa	13C3
Mount Pleasant	8G4
Mount Possession	10B5
Mount Somers	10B6
Mount Stoker	13E5
Mount Stuart	15F3
Mount Wesley	2B1
Mourea	3F4
Moutoa	7D2
Moutohora	4E4
Mt Aspiring	13B1
Mt Biggs	7E1
Mt Creighton	13A3
Mt Fyffe	9G3
Mt Nessing	11D6
Mt Nicholas	13A3
Muhunoa	7D2
Muhunoa East	7D3
Mukahanga	8G2
Murchison	8C6
Muriwai	4F6
Muriwai	6H1
Muriwai Beach	2C5
Murupara	3G5
Myross Bush	15B4

N

Naenae	7C5
Naike	3B2
Naperape	9F5
Napier	6E4
Naseby	13E3
National Park	5E3
Naumai	2B2
Neils Beach	12D3
Nelson	8E4
Nelson Creek	9A3
Nenthorn	13E5
Netherton	3D1
Netherwood	8F5
Neudorf	8E4
Nevis Crossing	13B4
New Brighton	10F5
New Creek	8B6
New Plymouth	5B2
Newbury	7E1
Newhaven	15F4
Newland	10D6
Newman	7E2
Newstead	3C3
Newton Flat	8C6

Ngaere	5B3
Ngahape	3C4
Ngahere	9A3
Ngahinapouri	3C3
Ngaiotonga	1F4
Ngakawau	8B5
Ngakonui	5E1
Ngakuru	3E5
Ngamatapouri	5D4
Ngamoku	5G6
Ngapaenga	3B5
Ngapara	13F3
Ngapeke	3F3
Ngapipito	1E5
Ngapuhi	1E5
Ngapuke	5E1
Ngapuna	13E5
Ngaputahi	3G6
Ngararatunua	1F6
Ngarimu Bay	2F6
Ngaroma	3D5
Ngaroto	3C3
Ngarua	3D2
Ngaruawahia	3C2
Ngataki	1B2
Ngatamahine	3B6
Ngatapa	4F6
Ngatea	3D1
Ngatimoti	8D4
Ngatira	3E4
Ngawaka	5F4
Ngawapurua	7F2
Ngawha	1E5
Ngawha Springs	1E5
Ngawihi	7D6
Ngongotaha	3F4
Ngongotaha Valley	3E4
Ngunguru	1G6
Ngutunui	3C4
Ngutuwera	5C5
Niagara	15D5
Nightcaps	14E5
Nihoniho	5D1
Nikau	7E2
Nikau	8B5
Nireaha	7E2
Nobles	9B3
Nokomai	13A5
Nonoti	9F5
Nopera	8G3
Normanby	5B4
Normanby	11E6
Norsewood	5G6
North Egmont	5B3
North River	2C1
North Taieri	13F6
Northope	15B4

Norton Reserve	13G2
Norwood	10E5
Notown	9A4
Nuhaka	6H2
Nukuhou North	3H4
Nukumaru	5D5
Nukuroa	13G2
Nukutawhiti	1E6

O

Oaklands	10E5
Oakleigh	1F6
Oakura	1F5
Oakura	5A2
Oamaru	13G3
Oaonui	5A3
Oaro	9G4
Ocean Beach	1G6
Ocean Beach	6F5
Ocean View	15G2
Oeo	5A4
Ohaeawai	1E4
Ohai	15A3
Ohakune	5E3
Ohangai	5B4
Ohapi	11E5
Ohau	7D5
Ohaua	3H6
Ohauiti	3E3
Ohaupo	3C3
Ohautira	3B3
Ohawe	5B4
Ohineakai	4G3
Ohinepaka	6F2
Ohinepanea	3G3
Ohinewai	3C2
Ohingaiti	5F5
Ohoka	10E4
Ohope	3H4
Ohotu	5F5
Ohura	5D1
Ohuri	1D5
Oio	5E2
Okaeria	3C1
Okahu	1C4
Okahu	2B1
Okahukura	5E1
Okaihau	1E4
Okains Bay	10G6
Okaiwa	5B4
Okaka	1D4
Okaramio	8G4
Okarito	11B2
Okato	5A2
Okau	5C1
Okauia	3E3
Okauia Pa	3E3

Ongaonga

Okere Falls	3F4
Okete	3B3
Okiato	1F4
Okiore	4D4
Okitu	4G6
Okiwi	2F2
Okiwi Bay	8F3
Okoia	5D5
Okoki	5C2
Okoroire	3D3
Okuku	10E4
Okupu	2F3
Okura	2D4
Okuru	12E2
Okuti Valley	10F6
Omaha	2D3
Omaha Flats	2D3
Omahu	2G6
Omahu	6E4
Omahuta	1D4
Omaio	4E3
Omaka Downs	8G5
Omakau	13D3
Omakere	6E6
Omamari	2A1
Omana	2B1
Omanaia	1D5
Omanawa	3E3
Omanu	3F2
Omanu Beach	3F2
Omapere	1C5
Omarama	13D1
Omarumutu	4E3
Omata	5A2
Omatane	5G5
Omaunu	1D4
Omiha	2E5
Omihi	9E6
Omimi	13F5
Omoana	5C3
Omokoroa	3E2
Omokoroa Beach	3E2
Omori	5F1
Omoto	10B1
Onaero	5B2
Onamalutu	8G5
One Tree Point	1F6
Onekaka	8D2
Onemana	2G6
Onepoto	6F1
Onepu	3G4
Onerahi	1F6
Oneriri	2C3
Oneroa	2E4
Onetangi	2E5
Onewhero	3B1
Ongaonga	5H5

Map Number/Co-ordinate

Ongarue

Ongarue	3C6
Ongaruru	4G4
Onoke	1D5
Opaea	5F4
Opaheke	2E6
Opahi	1E5
Opaki	7E3
Opaku	5C4
Opapa	6E5
Opape	4E3
Opara	1D5
Oparara	8B4
Oparau	3B4
Oparure	3B5
Opatu	5D2
Ophir	13D3
Opihi	11D5
Opiki	7D2
Opio	15B3
Opito	2G4
Oponae	4D4
Opononi	1C5
Oporo	15B4
Opotiki	4D3
Opou	8D1
Opouriao	3H4
Opoutama	6H2
Opouteke	1E6
Opoutere	2G6
Opua	1F4
Opuatia	3B1
Opuawhanga	1F5
Opuha	11D5
Opunake	5A4
Oraka Beach	6H2
Orakau	3C4
Orakeikorako	3E5
Orakipaoa	11E6
Orangimea	5D4
Oraora	1D5
Orapiu	2E5
Orari	11E5
Orari Bridge	11E5
Orautoha	5E3
Orawau	1D4
Orawia	15A3
Orepuki	15A4
Orere	2F5
Orere Point	2F5
Oreti Beach	15B4
Oreti Plains	15B3
Orewa	2D4
Oringi	7F1
Orini	3C2
Orinoco	8D4
Ormond	4F6
Ormondville	5G6

Oromahoe	1E4
Orongo	2F6
Orongo Bay	1F4
Oropi	3E3
Orton	11E5
Orua Bay	2D5
Orua Downs	7D1
Oruaiti	1D3
Oruaiti Beach	4F2
Oruaiwi	5E1
Oruanui	3E6
Oruawharo	2C2
Oruru	1D3
Osborne	13F6
Ostend	2E5
Ota Creek	15C4
Otaha	1E4
Otahei Bay	1F4
Otahu Flat	14E5
Otahuti	15B4
Otaika	1F6
Otaika Valley	1F6
Otaio	13G1
Otaio Gorge	13G1
Otairi	5E5
Otaitai Bush	15B4
Otakairangi	1F6
Otakeho	5B4
Otaki	7D3
Otaki Beach	7C3
Otaki Forks	7D3
Otakiri	3G4
Otakou	13F6
Otama	15C3
Otamakapua	5F5
Otamaroa	4F2
Otamauri	5H4
Otamita	15C3
Otane	3H5
Otane	6D5
Otangaroa	1D4
Otangiwai	3B6
Otanomomo	15F4
Otao	1E4
Otapiri	15B3
Otapiri Gorge	15B3
Otara	4D3
Otara	15D5
Otaraia	15D3
Otaramarae	3F4
Otatara	15B4
Otaua	1D5
Otaua	3B1
Otautau	15A3
Otehirinaki	4E3
Otekaieke	13F2
Otekura	15F4

Otematata	13E1
Oteramika	15C4
Otewa	3C4
Otiake	13F2
Otikerama	15D3
Otipua	11E6
Otira	9B5
Otiria	1E5
Otokia	15G2
Otoko	4E5
Otonga	1F5
Otoroa	1E3
Otorohanga	3C4
Otuhi	1F6
Otunui	5E1
Oturehua	13D3
Oturoa	3E4
Oturu	1C3
Otuwhare	4F3
Otway	3D2
Oue	1D5
Oueroa	6E6
Ouruhia	10F5
Outram	13E6
Overdale	10D6
Owaka	15F4
Owaka Valley	15E4
Oware	15D4
Oweka	8B6
Owen Junction	8C5
Owen River	8C5
Owhango	5E2
Owhata	1C4
Owhata	3F4
Owhiro	13E6
Owhiwa	1F6
Oxford	10D4

P

Paekakariki	7C4
Paenga	9C2
Paengaroa	3F3
Paepaerahi	3D4
Paerata	2E6
Paerata Ridge	3H4
Paerau	13D4
Paeroa	3D1
Paewhenua	3C5
Pahau	9E5
Pahautane	9A2
Pahi	2C2
Pahia	15A4
Pahiatua	7E2
Pahoia	3E2
Pahou	3H4
Paiaka	1F5
Paihia	1E4

Paremoremo

Pakanae	1D5
Pakaraka	1E4
Pakawau	8D1
Pakeho	3B5
Pakihikura	5F5
Pakipaki	6E5
Pakiri	2D2
Pakotai	1E6
Pakowhai	6E4
Palm Beach	2E4
Palmerston	13F5
Palmerston North	7E1
Pamapuria	1C4
Panetapu	3D4
Pangatotara	8D3
Panguru	1C5
Papaaroha	2F4
Papakai	5F2
Papakaio	13G3
Papakura	2E6
Papamoa	3F3
Papamoa Beach	3F3
Papanui Junction	5F4
Paparangi	5D5
Paparata	2E6
Paparimu	2E6
Paparoa	2C2
Paparore	1C3
Papatawa	7F1
Papatea	4F2
Papatoetoe	2D5
Papatotara	14E5
Papatowai	15E5
Papawai	7D4
Papawera	4G3
Paponga	1D4
Papua	1D5
Papueru	3G6
Para	8G4
Paradise	12D5
Parahi	2B2
Parakai	2C4
Parakao	1E6
Paranui	1D3
Paraoanui Pa	3H5
Parapara	1D3
Parapara	8D2
Paraparaumu	7C4
Paraparaumu Beach	7C3
Parau	2D5
Parawa	13A5
Parawai	2F6
Parawera	3C4
Parekarangi	3F5
Parekura Bay	1F4
Paremata	4G5
Paremoremo	2D4

Queenstown

Queenstown 13A3

R

Racecourse Hill 10D5
Raes Junction 13C6
Raetihi 5E3
Raglan 3B3
Rahotu 5A3
Rahui 8B6
Rai Valley 8F4
Rainbow Point 3E6
Raio 1C2
Rakahouka 15C4
Rakaia 10D6
Rakaia Huts 10E6
Rakau 8D4
Rakaumanga 3C2
Rakaunui 3B4
Rakauroa 4E5
Rakautao 1E5
Rakautara 9G3
Rakautatahi 5G6
Ramanui 5D3
Ramarama 2E6
Ranana 5D4
Ranfurly 13E3
Rangataua 5E3
Rangatira Valley 11E5
Rangi Point 1C5
Rangiahua 1D4
Rangiahua 6F2
Rangiaowhia 3C4
Rangiatea 3C4
Rangihaeata 8D2
Rangiora 10E4
Rangiotu 7D2
Rangipo 5F2
Rangipu 3B3
Rangiputa 1C3
Rangiriri 3C1
Rangiriri West 3C1
Rangitaiki 5H1
Rangitata 11E5
Rangitata Island 11E5
Rangitihi 1C4
Rangitoto 3C5
Rangitukia 4H3
Rangitumau 7E3
Rangiuru 3F3
Rangiwahia 5G5
Rankleburn 15E3
Ranui 2D5
Rapahoe 9A3
Rapaki 10F5
Rapanui 5D5
Rapaura 8G5
Rapuwai 11D5

Rarangi 8G4
Rata 5E6
Ratana 5E6
Ratanui 15E5
Ratapiko 5B3
Raukawa 5H5
Raukawa 6D5
Raukokore 4F2
Raumai 7E1
Raumati 7F1
Raumati Beach 7C4
Raumati South 7C4
Raupo 2B2
Raupo 9B3
Raupunga 6F2
Raurimu 5E2
Rawene 1D5
Rawhia 1D4
Rawhiti 1F4
Rawhitiroa 5B3
Raymonds Gap 15A3
Red Beach 2D4
Red Hill 2E6
Red Jacks 9A3
Redan 15D4
Redhill 2B2
Redruth 11E6
Redvale 2D4
Redwoods Valley 8E4
Reefton 9B2
Reena 1C5
Rehia 2B2
Rehutai 2A1
Reidston 13G3
Reikorangi 7C3
Remuera Settlement 1E5
Renown 3B2
Renwick 8G5
Reotahi Bay 1G6
Repia 2B2
Reporoa 3F5
Reporua 4H3
Rere 4E5
Rerewhakaaitu 3F5
Retaruke 5E2
Rewa 5F6
Rewanui 9A3
Rewarewa 3C5
Rewiti 2C4
Richmond 8E4
Richmond 13G3
Richmond Brook Stn 9H1
Richmond Downs 3D3
Richmond Heights 5G1
Rimu 15C4
Ringway 15A4
Riponui 1F5

Ripponvale 13B3
Rissington 6E4
Riverhead 2D4
Riverlands 8G5
Riverlea 5B3
Riversdale 15C2
Riversdale Beach 7F4
Riverside 11F5
Riverside 13E6
Riverton 15A4
Riwaka 8E3
Riwaka Valley 8E3
Roa 9A3
Rock and Pillar 13E4
Rockford 10D4
Rockville 8D2
Rokeby 10D6
Rolleston 10E5
Romahapa 15F4
Rongahere 15E3
Rongoiti Junction 5F5
Rongokokako 7E2
Rongomai 7E2
Rongotea 7D1
Roseberry 13G3
Rosedale 8E4
Rosewill 11E6
Roslyn Bush 15C4
Ross 10A3
Rossmore Stn 9H1
Rotherham 9E5
Rotoehu 3F4
Rotoiti 3F4
Rotokakahi 1C4
Rotokauri 3C3
Rotokautuku 4G3
Rotokawa 3E6
Rotokawa 3F4
Rotokino 11B1
Rotokohu 9B2
Rotomahana 3F5
Rotomanu 9B4
Rotongaro 3B2
Rotongata 3D4
Rotoorangi 3D3
Rotoroa 8D6
Rotorua 3F4
Rototuna 2B2
Rototuna 3C2
Rotowaro 3B2
Round Hill 15F3
Rowan 5B3
Roxburgh 13C5
Roxburgh East 13C5
Roxburgh Hydro 13C5
Ruahine 5F5
Ruahine 15A4

Seddon

Ruakaka 2C1
Ruakituri 4E6
Ruakokoputuna 7D5
Ruamahanga 2F5
Ruanui 5F4
Ruapekapeka 1F5
Ruapuke 3B3
Ruapuna 10B6
Ruarangi 2C1
Ruaroa 1C4
Ruaroa 7F1
Ruatahuna 3H6
Ruatangata West 1F6
Ruataniwha 5H6
Ruatapu 10A2
Ruatiti 5E3
Ruato 3F4
Ruatoki North 3H4
Ruatoria 4G3
Ruawai 2B2
Ruawaro 3B2
Ruawhata 7E2
Ruby Bay 8E4
Rukuhia 3C3
Rukuwai 1G6
Runanga 9A3
Runaruna 1C4
Runciman 2E6
Ruru 9A4
Russell 1F4
Russells Flat 10D4
Rutherglen 10B1
Ryal Bush 15B4

S

Saddle Hill 13F6
Saies 1D3
Salisbury 11E6
Saltwater Creek 10F4
Sandspit 2D3
Sandy Knolls 10E5
Sandymount 13F6
Sanson 7D1
Santoft 5E6
Scarborough 11E6
Scargill 9E5
Scotsman Valley 3D3
Scotts Gap 15A3
Scroggs Hill 15G2
Seacliff 13F5
Seadown 11E6
Seafield 11F4
Seaford 8D1
Seaforth 11E6
Seaview 10A2
Seaward Downs 15C4
Seddon 8H5

110

Seddonville

Tawharanui

Tawharemanuka

Tuamarina

Waipapakauri

Whatuwhiwhi

Whawharua

Yaldhurst

Y

AA Membership Information

If you are visiting New Zealand and are a member of an overseas motoring club, you are probably entitled to full reciprocal rights to the services detailed on this page. If you are not a member, you will be able to see the valuable range of services that membership gives you. Why not join now? If you are a member you are encouraged to make full use of the services which are in place to make motoring in New Zealand more pleasurable.

FREE AA emergency breakdown service

AA Emergency Breakdown Service is free to members, whether provided by AA Breakdown Service staff or an AA Breakdown Service Garage. Your AA membership covers the call-out, service and towing charges as a result of your vehicle breaking down or experiencing mechanical problems.

If your vehicle cannot be repaired on the spot, we'll arrange to tow your vehicle to the nearest AA Breakdown Service Garage for repair.

FREE touring maps

Whether touring, or just taking a short weekend trip, choose from a wide range of detailed AA Maps including personal itinerary guides, street maps, district maps and motorway guides.

FREE accommodation guides

North and South Island Accommodation Guides are available to AA members free of charge – giving you all the information you need to know, including tariffs, about all types of accommodation throughout New Zealand.

FREE technical advice

If you have any technical problems or queries involving your car, free advice is available to you by phone, letter or personal visit to any AA Technical Centre. This includes warranty disputes, faulty repair work and overcharging.

FREE legal assistance

If you receive a traffic infringement notice or have any legal problems associated with motoring, AA staff will advise you on procedures involved – free of charge. If appropriate you will be referred to the AA's solicitor and we will pay the first $55 of your legal costs.

FREE AA *Directions* magazine

Discover what's happening in the motoring and travel world today, and how it affects you, including consumer tests, car reviews, updates on motoring legislation and the latest in new car prices. AA *Directions* is delivered free to your home five times a year.

Road reports

Avoid unnecessary delays and frustration by checking road access and conditions before you set off. Simply call your nearest AA office for updated information and help on alternative routes. After hours please phone 0900 33 222 – calls cost $1 per minute.

World-wide reciprocal service

Our affiliation with the International Touring Alliance entitles you to advice and assistance from motoring organisations in more than 80 countries when travelling overseas.

AA member discounts

As part of New Zealand's largest member organisation you are now entitled to a range of special discounts at major sightseeing and retail outlets throughout New Zealand. Ask for details from your nearest AA Centre.

AA pre-purchase vehicle inspections

Get peace-of-mind used-car buying protection. Experienced AA Technical staff will carry out a comprehensive vehicle check. This exclusive check is available only to AA members at nominal cost.

AA Plus

An optional extra available to AA members (in addition to the AA membership subscription). A vehicle far from home developing a major fault or damage in an accident is transported back by a special vehicle-carrying truck.

If the mishap occurs more than 100km from home, an appropriate rental car may be provided (subject to compliance with renting conditions), with the AA reimbursing the member rental charges for a maximum of four days.

AA approved repairers

Take the risk out of choosing a reliable repair garage. Select with confidence garages displaying the AA Approved Repairer sign.

AA Driving School

Learn to drive with confidence with our special driver education programmes. You'll learn the right way with specific courses designed for you or members of your family.

AA Travel Service

Make the most of valuable holiday time with the knowledgeable help of our AA travel staff. For travel here or overseas, they'll put together the best value-for-money arrangements to suit your requirements, plus provide discount options where available.

Member finance

Investments in Registered Secured Debenture Stock, hire purchase for new or used vehicles, flexible mortgages for building, buying, renovating or home equity finance. Contact your nearest AA Centre.

AA Signs

AA Signs can manufacture, erect and maintain signs at competitive prices.

International driving permits

Obtainable at AA Centres for a nominal fee on production of a current NZ driver's licence and a passport-type photo.

AA merchandise

A wide range of motoring, travel and safety-related products are available at AA Centres, all with a minimum 10% discount for AA members.

AA Toll Free Emergency Breakdown Service Phone 0800 500 222